The Trivia Lovers'
Guide To

FOOTBALL

The Trivia Lovers'
Guide To

FOOTBALL

First published in 2007
Reprinted in 2009

Packaged by Susanna Geoghegan HP2 6HG
Cover and design by Peter Wilkinson
Typeset by David Onyett, Publishing & Production Services, Cheltenham
Printed in China

Introduction

When the great Bill Shankly famously remarked 'Some people think football is a matter of life and death. I don't take that attitude. I can assure them it is much more serious than that', fans everywhere nodded their heads in agreement.

Football is not only 'the beautiful game' played at the 'Theatre of Dreams' and other equally evocative stadiums around the world, it has been a source of speculation, debate and endless fascination for centuries. From the rough and tumble of medieval streets where mobs pursued an inflated pig's bladder, to the playing fields of England's 19th-century public schools; from Sunday League recreation grounds, to the hallowed turf of the world's leading clubs today, football has gripped the imagination and fired the passions of generations of players and supporters.

Along the way it has collected an absorbing array of facts, figures and feats on and off the field, which form the raw material for this collection of assorted football records and recollections. Gathered in the following pages are accounts of memorable matches, celebrated players, inspirational managers, and a few of the less august (but equally memorable) events that have contributed to the rich lore of football.

FOOTBALL

Historic Footballing Firsts

The first game between a British side and an American side is thought to have been the match between Yale University and the touring Eton Players on 6 December 1873 in New Haven. Yale won 2–1.

The first team to win the FA Cup three times in a row were Wanderers. They won three finals from 1876 to 1878 beating Old Etonians, Oxford University and the Royal Engineers.

Football first became popular in Spain in the Basque region, through the influence of migrant British workers in the 1890s. Clubs such as Athletic Bilbao still have their English names as a result.

Football was introduced into Moscow by an English mill owner, Clem Charnock who showed the game to his Russian workers in 1887. With other relatives, Charnock created his own team – called 'Morozovtsi' after the name of the mill – which became one of the best sides in Russia for many years. The first club in Russia was thought to have been the St Petersburg Football Club founded in 1879, though this was created by and for British residents in the city and Russians were discouraged from joining.

The first winners of the League were Preston North End who claimed the inaugural championship in 1889

without losing one of their 22 games and drawing only
four. They also won the FA Cup that year without
conceding a goal. Little wonder that the Preston team
of that era earned the name 'The Invincibles'. In 1903,
Bury too won the Cup without letting in a goal.

The great Italian football team Juventus first sported
their famous wear black and white stripes after seeing
English side Notts County play in 1903.

The first world football rankings were probably those
that appeared in 1933 from the pen of a Hungarian
football writer. This placed Austria in top position with
Scotland second followed by England then Italy.

The great Manchester City player Frank Swift, who
won his first cap in 1946, was the first goalkeeper to
captain England. His brother Fred Swift was also a
goalkeeper who played for Oldham. Frank died in the
1958 Munich air disaster, when he was travelling on
the plane as a journalist.

When Norman Hunter stepped onto the pitch for
England against Spain on 8 December 1965 he became
the first England player to make his debut as a
substitute.

The first player to be capped by England while playing
for a foreign team was Gerry Hitchens. The former

FOOTBALL

Aston Villa player turned out for Inter Milan and a number of other Italian clubs between 1961 and 1970. He played seven times for England and scored five international goals.

The first major football tournament won on penalties was the 1976 European Championship. The winners were Czechoslovakia. Ironically their defeated opponents were West Germany whose team were later to gain a reputation for winning penalty shoot-outs – especially against England.

Needs Must

Reading showed how resourceful football clubs can be when they really want to win a game. Faced with an 1893–94 FA Cup qualifying tie at home to Southampton St Mary's, Reading naturally wanted to field their strongest team, including a player called Jimmy Stewart. The snag was that Stewart, who was in the army at Aldershot, was being held in detention in a guardroom and was therefore unavailable. Until, that is, an enterprising Reading official plied the officer in charge of the guardroom with drink and got the player released for the match. Stewart duly scored the crucial goal in Reading's 2–1 win. Southampton later protested when news of the subterfuge came out, but the FA ruled that no regulations had been broken.

Still Reading perhaps got their come-uppance in the first round proper of the Cup – losing 18–0 to Preston North End.

Pioneering Instinct

Southampton have a strong tradition of adventure when it comes to touring. In 1901 the Saints toured abroad for the first time and visited Belgium, Austria and Hungary. They won all six matches scoring 44 goals in all and conceding just three. In the 1903–04 season Southampton were the first English team to tour Argentina and in 1948 became the first English team to tour Brazil.

City and United Beware

'That wheeas there has been heretofore great disorders in our town of Manchester, and the inhabitants thereof greatly wronged and charged with makinge and amendinge of their glasse windows broken yearelye and spoyled by a companye of lewd and disordered persons using the unlawful exercise if playinge with the ffote-ball in ye streets of ye sd towne breakinge many men's windowes and lasse at their pleasures and other great enormities. Therefore we of this jurye doe order that no manner of persons herefatre shall play or use the ffote-ball in any street within the said towne of Manchester.'

From a Manchester Lete Roll of 1608

FOOTBALL

Victory Guaranteed

On the final day of Italy's Serie B season, Genoa won promotion to Serie A after a 3–2 victory over Venezia. However, celebrations in Genoa were short-lived when it came to light that Venezia had been given $300,000 before the match to ensure that Genoa would win. Genoa's president and general manager were given five-year suspensions from the game for match-fixing and two Venezia players were banned for six months. As for Genoa's promotion, that was reversed to demotion to Serie C.

View from the Terraces

'The natural state of the football fan is bitter disappointment, no matter what the score.'

Nick Hornby

What's in a Name?

Manchester United only took on their current name in 1902. Founded in 1878, the club was originally called Lancashire & Yorkshire Railway Newton Heath before that quickly became just Newton Heath.

One of the most unusual names for an existing professional football club belonged to Bristol Rovers. When they were created in 1883 they were originally called the Black Arabs. This name came from their black shirts – and the name of a rugby side called the Arabs who played on a nearby pitch. They later became Eastville Rovers before adopting their current name in 1898.

The Uruguayan club of Peñarol was founded in 1891 when it was known as The Central Uruguay Railway Cricket Club, taking both its name and its colours of gold and black from the local railway company.

The Czech club Sparta Prague were originally called King's Vineyard when they were founded in 1893, but soon changed their name to 'Sparta' in honour of one of the ancient Greek city-states whose inhabitants were noted for their discipline and military prowess.

Manchester City were called West Gorton St Marks when they were created in 1880 changing to Ardwick FC in 1887 and finally to Manchester City in 1894.

The great Spanish team Real Madrid had its royal label ('Real' is Spanish for 'Royal') awarded it by King Alfonso XIII on 29 June 1920. The King was a keen football fan who had been honorary president of the Spanish Football Association – upon whom he bestowed the title Royal on 30 July 1913.

The Finnish team FC Jazz was founded in 1934 under

the name of Porin Pallo–Toveritand (PPT). Their current name comes from the fact that they are based in Pori, home to an annual jazz festival.

The football club Atlante, from Mexico City, at one time called themselves U–53 in honour of a German U–boat.

Voting with their Feet

India withdrew from the 1950 World Cup in protest at the rule requiring players to wear boots.

A Day to Remember

When Arbroath beat Aberdeen side Bon Accord 36–0 in the first round of the Scottish Cup on 12 September 1885, it was said that the Arbroath goalkeeper Jim Milne did not touch the ball during the game. In fact, his biggest problem seems to have been the rain – according to reports he sheltered under a spectator's brolly for part of the game.

The explanation for the heavy defeat may lie in the fact that the Scottish FA invited the wrong team to take part in the competition. They should have asked Orion FC from Aberdeen to play, but instead asked Orion Cricket Club. The cricketers were nothing if not game, and so decided to play – under the name Bon Accord.

Bon Accord waived their home advantage for the match for the very good reason they didn't have a pitch of their own and chose to play away. Incredibly, on the same day, Dundee Harp beat Aberdeen Rangers 35–0 in the same competition.

England Expects

In 1909 the England players were forced by the FA to sign a statement saying they were determined to win in the forthcoming Home Championship. This strange occurrence came against a backdrop of industrial unrest. There had been controversy in England when the FA decided not to recognize the Players' Union founded two years earlier.

Eventually the FA backed down after a players' strike. Unfortunately, in a statement reassuring the public that the Home Championship would go ahead, the Union said that England would play and at the same time 'do their utmost to win'. In the fevered atmosphere at the time this was wrongly interpreted in the media, and by many fans, as suggesting that the players had actually considered trying to lose.

In order to clarify the situation the FA made the players sign a statement making clear their commitment to winning – which they did convincingly by beating Ireland, Wales and Scotland without conceding a goal.

FOOTBALL

Penalty Spree

On 29 March 1989 the Second Division game between Crystal Palace and Brighton achieved notoriety when referee Kelvin Morton awarded five penalties in the space of 27 minutes. Only two were converted, with each side claiming one apiece and Crystal Palace emerging with a 2–1 victory.

The sequence of events in this extraordinary game began when Crystal Palace were leading 1–0. Brighton, down to ten men, had conceded a penalty which was taken by Mark Bright who succeeded in finding the net, giving Palace a 2–0 lead.

Only a matter of minutes later Morton awarded Palace a second penalty, but this time the Brighton goalkeeper, John Keeley, brought off a fine save, to keep the score at 2–0.

Still within five minutes of the first penalty, Kelvin Morton awarded Palace their third. This time Ian Wright placed the ball on the spot to try his luck. His luck was out and he missed. Two potential goals had gone begging and the score remained 2–0.

Half-time came and play continued for ten minutes into the second half before Brighton were awarded a penalty. Responsibility for the spot kick went to Alan

Curbishley, who powered the ball into the Palace net. The score moved to 2–1.

The final penalty of the game went to Crystal Palace and John Pemberton took on the job of making it 3–1. However, he missed as well, and what could have been a thumping 5–1 Palace victory stayed at a 2–1 win.

World Cup Golden Boot Winners

In every World Cup competition, the player with the highest tally of goals in the finals is awarded the golden boot. To date they are as follows.

Year	Player	Country	Goals
1930	Guillermo Stábile	Argentina	8
1934	*Oldrich Nejedly	Czechoslovakia	5
1938	Leônidas da Silva	Brazil	8
1950	Marques Ademir	Brazil	7
1954	Sandor Kocsis	Hungary	11
1958	Just Fontaine	France	13
1962	Flórián Albert	Hungary	4
"	Garrincha	Brazil	"
"	Valentin Ivanov	USSR	"
"	Drazen Jerkovic	Yugoslavia	"
"	Leonel Sánchez	Chile	"
"	Vavá	Brazil	"
1966	Eusébio	Portugal	9

1970	Gerd Müller	Germany	10
1974	Grzegorz Lato	Poland	7
1978	Mario Kempes	Argentina	6
1982	Paolo Rossi	Italy	6
1986	Gary Lineker	England	6
1990	Salvatore Schillaci	Italy	6
"	Oleg Salneko	Russia	"
1994	Hristo Stoichkov	Bulgaria	6
1998	Davor Suker	Croatia	6
2002	Ronaldo	Brazil	8
2006	Miroslav Klose	Germany	5

*In 2006 FIFA revised Oldrich Nejedly's 1934 tally to five goals, which made him the outright winner of the golden boot for the second World Cup. Prior to that he had shared the award with Edmund Conen (Germany) and Angelo Schiavio (Italy) with four goals apiece.

German Victory: 1966

The first German side to win a European trophy were Borussia Dortmund. They beat Liverpool 2–1 after extra time in the final of the Cup Winners Cup at Hampden Park, Glasgow on 5 May 1966.

More in Hope than Expectation

Any one picking up a programme for a 1974 FA Cup tie involving a replay between Plymouth Argyle and

Manchester United would have been puzzled if they searched the record books to discover the result. The game never took place. United had already beaten the Devon side 1–0 in the Cup tie at old Trafford. Argyle had simply printed the programme well in advance as a precaution in those days of power cuts and the three-day week.

Limited Liabilty

Birmingham City began life in 1875 as Small Heath Allliance, formed by a group of cricketers from Holy Church in Bordesley Green. They became known as Birmingham in 1905. In 1888 – while still called Small Heath Alliance – they became the first club to adopt limited liability. The share capital of the club was £650.

White-out

The freezing weather of the 1962–3 winter took its toll on scheduled football matches, along with many other aspects of national life. As far as the English and Scottish leagues were concerned, the worst day of that prolonged spell of bitterly cold weather was 9 February 1963. This was the day when 57 games were postponed because of snow and ice. In all, only seven Football League games could be played and those were all south of the border; in Scotland, the entire Scottish League programme had to be cancelled.

FOOTBALL

For three consecutive Saturdays in January 1962 the
Football Pools coupons were declared void. Bolton
Wanderers suffered the longest period in League history
without playing a match. After their 1–0 win over Spurs
on 8 December 1962, they were unable to take to the field
again until 16 February, when they lost 3–2 to Arsenal.

Football Politics

'What was interesting was that virtually all the leaders –
because there wasn't a huge burning issue, actually at
the council – were standing around talking about
football in the corridors.'

Tony Blair

A Safe Pair of Hands

The great England goalkeeper Gordon Banks kept 35
clean sheets in his 73 appearances for his country.
During 1966 he went seven games in a row without
letting the ball past him, until Eusebio beat him with a
penalty in the World Cup semi-final.

Bombs Away

The creation of Stirling Albion Football Club came
about as the result of miscalculations by the crew of a
Second World War German bomber. On its way home
after an air raid on the River Clyde in July 1940, the

aircraft jettisoned its remaining bomb over the quiet town of Stirling and its picturesque Old Forthbank ground. By a sad irony, only two bombs fell on Stirling during the entire war, but this one demolished the Forthbank grandstand, flattened part of the terracing, and left a 6m deep crater in the pitch. The King's Park Football Club, which had made its home at Forthbank, crumbled under the onslaught, so ending one football era but heralding another.

As the war came to a close, a local consortium, led by coal magnate, Tom Ferguson, came up with a plan to rebuild and relocate the club at Annfield Park; and in 1945 Stirling Albion was formed. In 1971 the club was managed by Bob Shankly, whose brother Bill was manager at that other Anfield in Liverpool.

Second Best

Sir Alf Ramsey, the only manager to win a World Cup for England, was not even first choice for the job before he took over in 1963. After the departure of Walter Winterbottom in 1962, the position was first offered to Winterbottom's assistant Jimmy Adamson. Adamson, from Burnley, declined the post because he didn't want to spend so much time away from home in his beloved north of England. So the job went to Alf Ramsey who, soon after taking the post, predicted that England would win the 1966 World Cup.

FOOTBALL

Players of the Century

As the end of the last millennium approached, the IFFHS (International Federation of Football History and Statistics) conducted a worldwide survey to identify the best football players of the 20th century. The top 50 outfield players were listed as follows. There was a separate list for goalkeepers (which follows later in this book) and also a separate list of the world's top women football players (which will also be found later).

1	Pelé	Brazil
2	Johan Cruijff	Netherlands
3	Franz Beckenbauer	Germany
4	Alfredo di Stéfano	Argentina
5	Diego Armando Maradona	Argentina
6	Ferenc Puskás	Hungary
7	Michel Platini	France
8	Garrincha	Brazil
9	Eusébio	Portugal
10	Robert Charlton	England
11	Stanley Matthews	England
12	Marco van Basten	Netherlands
13	Gerd Müller	Germany
14	Zico	Brazil
15	Lothar Matthäus	Germany
16	George Best	Northern Ireland
17	Juan Alberto Schiaffino	Uruguay
18	Ruud Gullit	Netherlands

19	Valdir Pereira Didi	Brazil
"	Gianni Rivera	Italy
21	Giuseppe Meazza	Italy
22	Matthias Sindelar	Austria
23	Fritz Walter	Germany
24	Robert Moore	England
25	José Manuel Moreno	Argentina
26	Hugo Sánchez	Mexico
27	George Weah	Liberia
28	Roger Milla	Cameroon
29	José Leonardo Andrade	Uruguay
30	Just Fontaine	France
"	Francisco Gento	Spain
32	Ladislao Kubala	Spain
33	Franco Baresi	Italy
34	Josef Bican	Czechoslovakia
35	Karl-Heinz Rummenigge	Germany
36	Omar Sivori	Argentina
37	Elias Figueroa	Chile
38	Kevin Keegan	England
39	Sándor Kocsis	Hungary
40	Héctor Scarone	Uruguay
41	Josef Masopust	Czechoslovakia
42	Giacchinto Facchetti	Italy
43	Raymond Kopa	France
"	Alessandro Mazzola	Italy
45	Uwe Seeler	Germany
46	Gunnar Nordahl	Sweden
47	Zizinho	Brazil

48	Teófilo Cubillas	Peru
49	Arsenio Erico	Paraguay
50	Denis Law	Scotland

Beginners' Luck

Some debuts go better than others. Harold Halse scored a goal within 30 seconds of his first game for Manchester United in March 1908. Charles Sagar hadn't got on the score sheet quite so quickly on his United debut three year ealier in 1905 – but he did manage a hat-trick against Bristol City. Neil Webb scored a goal on his United debut in four different competitions – the FA and League Cups, the League and in the Cup-Winners' Cup. Oddly, these were out of a total of only eleven goals that he scored for the club. David Herd scored on his United debut in five competitions – including three European competitions – but failed to score on his United League debut.

Third Division International

In 1947 Third Division Notts County achieved a remarkable coup in signing the England centre-forward, Tommy Lawton from Chelsea for a record fee of £20,000. As a result of this transfer, Lawton became the first England international to play his club football outside the top two divisions.

The Busby Record

Sir Matt Busby earned his undying fame as a great manager for Manchester United from 1945 to 1971, but before the Second World War he had played six years for Manchester City and four years for United's other great rivals Liverpool, where he was captain. During the Second World War Busby made three appearances for Chelsea as well as turning out for Middlesbrough, Reading, Brentford, Bournemouth & Boscombe Athletic and Hibs.

Team Spirit

'There are two great teams on Merseyside; Liverpool and Liverpool Reserves.'

Bill Shankly

Football Formations

2-3-5
The traditional formation for outfield players (originally known as the pyramid) with five players up front: two on the wings, two playing as inside-forwards and a centre-forward. Behind them were three half-backs and two full-backs.

4-4-2/4-3-3
Two formations covering the outfield players. In 4-4-2,

the side will play with four defenders, four midfielders and two strikers. In 4-3-3, one of the midfield players becomes a third striker.

Christmas Tree

This is a modern formation which usually has four backs, three midfield players, two supporting strikers and a lone lead striker. When viewed from above, the formation looks like a Christmas tree.

Diamond

A formation that has the outfield players lining up with two strikers, a third striker just behind them and in front of two midfield players, a third midfield player just behind them and in front of four defenders. The strength of this formation is that the four defenders have a supporting player, as do the two strikers. Its weakness is that most of the players are based in the central area of the field, giving little or no width.

Zone Defence

A defensive formation in which each player is assigned a specific area of the field to defend, so irrespective of who comes into that zone, the defender is expected to deal with the threat. If more than one player comes into the zone, then a defender from the neighbouring zone is expected to move across to lend support, although at the same time this creates space in another zone that could be exploited.

Running Repairs

Partick Thistle won the Scottish Cup on 16 April 1921 against Rangers, thanks to right-winger John Blair who scored the only goal of the match. His marker, left-back James Bowie, was off the field at the time – changing a pair of ripped shorts.

Scottish Football Association

The Scottish Football Association was founded on 13 March, 1873, at a meeting at Dewar's Hotel in Glasgow. The eight founding clubs were:

Clydesdale
Dumbreck
Eastern
Granville
Queen's Park
Kilmarnock
Third Lanark
Vale of Leven

Famous Five

The Irish midfielder Johnny Giles was the first man to appear in five FA Cup Wembley finals, once with Manchester United in 1963, and four times with Leeds United, 1965, 1970, 1972 and 1973.

FOOTBALL

Mass Exodus

Czechoslovakia swept all before them as they stormed through to the soccer final of the 1920 Olympic Games in Antwerp. However, things came a little unstuck after that. They were 2–0 down to Belgium after 39 minutes, and dismayed at what they saw as biased refereeing, the entire Czechoslovak team walked off the field. They were disqualified, which meant they didn't even get the silver medal – which went to Spain.

Triple Record-holder

The prolific striker Ted MacDougall became the first player to be the leading goal-scorer in three different divisions. This was with Bournemouth & Boscombe Athletic in the Fourth Division in 1970–71, and in the Third Division in 1971–72, and then with Norwich in the First Division in the 1975–76. In the course of this MacDougall scored 103 goals for Bournemouth in 146 games during his first spell with the club, including nine which he claimed against hapless Margate in a first round FA Cup tie that Bournemouth won 11–0.

Mistaken Identity

Swapping your shirt after a big match can have its drawbacks. Dave Webb, Chelsea's inspirational defender, exchanged a shirt with a Leeds United player after the Blues had won the exciting FA Cup final replay 2–1 at Old Trafford on 29 April 1970. Unfortunately, an official stopped Webb from going up to the directors' box to collect his medal – as the official thought Webb was a Leeds player.

Olympic Mayhem

The simple occurrence of a referee disallowing a 'goal' on 24 May 1964 led to the deaths of 318 people. With just two minutes to go as Peru played Argentina in a crucial Olympic qualifying match in Lima, the ref disallowed the goal that would have sent the home team to the Games in Tokyo. The largely Peruvian crowd was incensed and the massive riot that ensued in the National Stadium led to the unprecedented death toll – and injuries to at least 500 more people.

Battle Of Highbury

The match between Italy and England at Highbury on 14 November 1934 was billed by the Italians as the most important match played anywhere since the 1914–18 war. Fascist leader Benito Mussolini offered each of his players £150 and an Alfa Romeo sports car if they won, such was his determination for an Italian victory.

This may explain why the match became one of the

most violent internationals ever played. The so-called Battle of Highbury was largely blamed on the Italians, who it was said were looking to kick 'everybody and anything' in sight. The Italians claimed that an injury to their centre-half in the opening minutes had been deliberate. In any event the game was full of blood-curdling tackles, punches and elbows to the face.

After the match, which England won 3–2, the FA even considered pulling out of future internationals. One newspaper by-lined its report of the match 'By Our War Correspondent'.

Referee's Assistants

These are officials who patrol the touchline, indicating to which side a throw-in should be awarded, not to mention offsides and other offences that might otherwise be missed by the referee. Originally called linesmen, because they patrolled the line, they were upgraded to assistant referee status in the 1990s. This despite a trial international match in 1935 when the linesmen were dispensed with in favour of two referees; although the pair who officiated in this manner delivered a glowing report on the system's advantages, the FA Council decided to keep linesmen. For nearly 50 years linesmen were paid exactly half the match fee the referee received.

Club Colours

'It is a good plan, if it can previously be so arranged, to have one side with striped jerseys of one colour, say red; and the other with another, say blue. This prevents confusion and wild attempts to run after and wrest the ball from your neighbour. I have often seen this done, and heard the invariable apology – "I beg your pardon, I thought you were on the opposite side."

Routledge's Handbook of Football, 1867

20th-century Goalkeepers

According to the IFFHS ((International Federation of Football History and Statistics) survey conducted at the end of the last millennium the top 20 goalkeepers in the 20th century were:

1	Lev Yashin	Soviet Union
2	Gordon Banks	England
3	Dino Zoff	Italy
4	Sepp Maier	Germany
5	Ricardo Zamora	Spain
6	José Luis Félix Chilavert	Paraguay
7	Peter Schmeichel	Denmark
8	Peter Shilton	England
9	Frantisek Plánicka	Czechoslovakia
10	Amadeo Raúl Carrizo	Argentina
11	Gilmar dos Santos Neves	Brazil

12	Ladislao Mazurkiewicz	Uruguay
13	Patrick Jennings	Northern Ireland
14	Ubaldo Matildo Fillol	Argentina
15	Antonio Carbajal	Mexico
16	Jean-Marie Pfaff	Belgium
17	Rinat Dasaev	Soviet Union
18	Gyula Grosics	Hungary
19	Thomas Ravelli	Sweden
20	Walter Zenga	Italy

Optional Extras: Goal Nets

Patented by J. A. Brodie of Liverpool in 1890, these were tested for the first time in a match at Bolton. After the FA had interviewed Mr Brodie and conducted a trial, they were happy to approve their use but, since they were not able to guarantee the price Mr Brodie could charge clubs, they did not amend their rules to make them compulsory. Even though they appear at every ground, they are still optional according to the rules.

Welsh Wizardry

One of the older football clubs in Wales, Bangor City won the Welsh Cup in 1961–2 which earned them entry into the European Cup Winners' Cup for the first time. However, they looked like making a swift exit after the draw was announced and they found themselves lined up against the winners of the Italian Cup, Napoli, which was one of the leading teams in Europe at the time.

Bangor played the first leg of the tie at their home ground, Farrar Road, and against all expectations won the game 2–0. Three weeks later they found themselves in southern Italy taking to the field in front of 80,000 die-hard Napoli fans. This time the Italian team emerged the winners, with a final 3–1 score line. Had the modern away-goal ruling been in force then, Bangor would have progressed to the second round. As it was, the tie was drawn 3–3 and a playoff was required. This was held at Highbury, the first time that Arsenal's home ground had hosted a European Cup Winner's Cup tie. Another desperately close encounter ensued and with the score 1–1 inside the last ten minutes of the game, Bangor must surely have felt that their luck was holding out. That was until Napoli scored the winning goal seven minutes from full-time and ended Bangor City's giant-killing aspirations.

Abandon all Hope of Further Play

A match that is brought to a halt before the end of the full 90 minutes is described as being 'abandoned'. While the weather is the most usual reason for calling an early end to any match, there have been a wide variety of reasons over the years ranging from crowd trouble and pitch invasions, players fighting among themselves, fans ripping down the goalposts and there not being any replacements, players dying midway through a match, floodlight failure, fires in the stands during the game, a flooded pitch and teams refusing to take to the field for the second half. During the Second World War, numerous wartime League fixtures were abandoned owing to air raids or warnings!

Football Pools

In 1922 the first football pool was established in a one-room office at 28 Martineau Street, Birmingham. Pari-Mutual Pools was established by a former Coldstream Guards officer named John Jervis Barnard. His first coupon had a single pool with six teams to win and so few coupons were returned that their combined proceeds did not cover the postage costs. Barnard was close to abandoning the scheme but decided to give it a last try at the start of the following football season. This time the response was more encouraging and coupons continued to be returned in sufficient numbers for him to keep Jervis Pools (as the firm was renamed) going until 1938, when Barnard sold out to David Cope of Cope's Pools.

Jervis Pools may not have generated the kind of turnover and profits its creator might have hoped, but his idea sowed seeds of interest with others, among them a 26-year-old telegraphist at the Commercial Cable Co's Liverpool station named John Moores. Moores and a couple of colleagues had become interested in a Jervis coupon they had found, to the extent that they spent time calculating how many coupons needed to be distributed before they returned a profit. The number they arrived at was 4,000. Taking the idea a stage further, they had a coupon of their own printed under the pseudonym 'Littlewood' – to disguise their identities and protect their jobs. Boys were hired to distribute 4,000 coupons outside the Manchester United Football Stadium and the founders of Littlewoods waited to see what return they achieved. The answer was 35 coupons with a total stake of £4 7 shillings and 6 pence, from which the first dividend of £2 12 shillings had to be paid. John Moores' partners baled out soon after, but he stuck with the idea and made his first million pounds within seven years.

Before the Second World War the highest premium paid went to R. Levy of London, who won £30,780 with four wins in April 1937. Thirteen years later Mrs Knowlson of Manchester became the first six-figure winner when she scooped £104,990 on 7 November 1950. Twenty-two years after her, Cyril Grimes of Liss in Hampshire became the first person to win half a million pounds as an individual British football-pool prize, when his coupon earned him £512,683 on 4 March 1972.

FOOTBALL

It took another six year before the first £1 million was won by a single pools coupon and this belonged to a syndicate of nine nurses and two hospital workers in Devizes, Wiltshire. Between them they shared £1, 017, 890, though their patients had a hand in the win as it had been they who had chosen the winning numbers.

World Cup History

The Coupe Jules Rimet, the beautiful trophy awarded for winning the World Cup, had an eventful existence. Legend has it that during the Second World War the Italian vice-president of FIFA, Ottorino Barassi, hid the hallowed trophy from advancing occupying troops in a shoebox.

It was then stolen twice. The first theft was in 1966 in England, but the trophy was later recovered after being found by a dog called Pickles. However, the trophy, whose base was made of lapis lazuli and was created by French sculptor Abel Lafleur, was stolen again in Rio de Janeiro in 1983 and is thought to have been melted down.

Beaten Men

In the run-up to the 15th World Cup, staged in the USA in 1994, Macao played six games in the Asian group, lost all six, scored no goals, but conceded 46.

Abiding by the Amateur Code

The strict rules governing the amateur status of football players in the 1890s led to Eddie Payne almost losing his accreditation as an amateur because of a row that blew up over his football boots.

Payne, who had been neglected as a player at Fulham in 1892, made his debut for Spurs in 21 October 1893. Going to collect his kit from Fulham, he found that it had been stolen. Spurs were able to kit him out with everything he needed except a pair of boots, so he was given ten shillings to buy a new pair himself. After his first match against Old St Marks in a London FA Cup tie, Fulham accused Spurs of having poached their player and made further charges of professionalism.

The London FA felt moved to investigate the allegations and ruled that, while Spurs were not guilty of having poached Payne, they had broken the rules as far as his status as an amateur were concerned. In order to retain this, Eddie Payne was made to repay his ten-shilling boot money.

Lisbon Lions

This was the name given to the 11 Celtic players who became the first British football team to lift the European Cup when they defeated Inter Milan 2–1 in the final played at the National Stadium in Portugal. Apart from being the first team from northern Europe to win the coveted trophy, Celtic had the added distinction that all 11 players came from the club's home city of Glasgow. They were:

Ronnie Simpson	Goalkeeper
Jim Craig	Right back
Tommy Gemmell	Left back
Bobby Murdoch	Right-sided mid-fielder
Billy McNeill (captain)	Centre back
John Clark	Sweeper
Jimmy Johnstone	Outside right
Willie Wallace	Inside right
Stevie Chalmers	Centre forward
Bertie Auld	Inside left
Bobby Lennox	Outside left

Losing Hat-trick

It isn't often that a team is awarded four penalties in the same game; it's rarer still for it to miss three of them. But this is precisely what happened to Burnley during their Division II game against Grimsby Town on 13 February 1909. When the Grimsby goalkeeper, W. Scott, saved a hat-trick of penalties his colleagues must have fancied their chances, even though Burnley were a goal up. Then came the fourth penalty and this was beyond even Scott's heroics. As the ball powered past him into the net, it gave Burnley a 2–0 lead and that is how the score remained when the final whistle was blown.

The Philosophy of Football

Albert Camus the great French writer and existential philosopher, who died in 1960, was a very keen football player and appeared in goal for an Algerian XI. He once said about his work: 'All I know for certain about the morality and the obligations of men is that I owe it to football.'

Women Footballers of the 20th Century

According to the IFFHS ((International Federation of Football History and Statistics) survey conducted at the end of the last millennium the top 30 women players of the 20th century were:

1	Mia Hamm	USA
2	Michelle Akers	USA
3	Heidi Mohr	Germany
4	Carolina Morace	Italy
5	Sissi	Brazil
6	Linda Medalen	Norway
7	Liu Ailing	China
8	Kristine Lilly	USA
9	Heidi Støre	Norway

FOOTBALL

10	Pia Sundhage	Sweden
11	Joulie Foudy	USA
12	Gao Hong	China
13	Silvia Neid	Germany
14	Joy Fawcett	USA
15	Elisabetta Vignotto	Italy
16	Helge Riise	Norway
17	Bettina Wiegmann	Germany
18	Sun Qing-Mei	China
19	Pretinha	Brazil
20	Martina Voss	Germany
21	Gro Espeseth	Norway
"	Lena Videkull	Sweden
23	Ann Kristin Aarønes	Norway
24	Charmaine Hooper	Canada
"	Gunn Nyborg	Norway
26	Carin Gabarra-Jennings	USA
"	Fan Yunjie	China
28	Anette Börjesson	Sweden
29	Doris Fitschen	Germany
30	Alicia Vargas	Mexico

Winging it

'Ryan Giggs is one of those rare players who could play football in a phone box and find the door no matter how many players were in there with him.'

Carlos Queiroz

The Italian Job

The great Italian football club AC Milan came into being barely a fortnight before the beginning of the 20th century. As the club's English-language website has it, the club was established on 16 December 1899, 'its parents being three Englishmen Kilpin, Allison and Davies. They came to the idea when they were at a pint of beer, and they proposed it to two businessmen, Edwards and Nathan, and to another person, Mr Barnett.'

What they were proposing was the creation of the Milan Cricket and Football Club, with the aim of playing 'cricket as much as they could and to promote the game of football, not so popular in those times.'

Kilpin skippered the newly formed team, with Allison and Davies also turning out to play for the club's first fixture: a 3–0 win over Kilpin's former club Mediolanum. In fact the Milan team sheet that day contained other players with British names: Hoode, Lees and Neville.

UEFA

The Union of European Football Associations was formed in 1954 and almost immediately announced plans for the formation of the Champion Clubs Cup, or

FOOTBALL

European Cup as it was more commonly known. This was launched in 1955, with Real Madrid of Spain winning the first five competitions. The competition was replaced by the UEFA Champions League for the 1992-93 season. Despite the name, not every entrant is their country's reigning League champions; when Manchester United won the competition in 1999, they had only finished second behind Arsenal in the Premier League the previous season. England currently has four entrants into each competition – two qualify automatically, while the remaining two have to enter the play-off stage. UEFA also organised the European Cup Winners' Cup, held between 1961 and 1999, and the European Championships for national sides, which has been held every four years since 1960.

The UEFA Cup competition replaced the Inter-Cities Fairs Cup in 1971. In England entry is now given to the two sides that win the League Cup and FA Cup (unless either of these sides qualify for the Champions League), and those clubs finishing in fifth and sixth place in the Premiership. In the case of the FA Cup, if the winning side has already qualified for the Champions League, then entry will be given to the runners-up. Additionally, UEFA also award an extra place to the side throughout Europe that finishes top of the fair play chart but did not qualify for Europe via its League placing.

Originally organised on a straight knockout basis, with clubs playing each other home and away, it now has a qualifying knockout phase, a mini group stage and then reverts back to a knockout stage, with unsuccessful sides from the Champions League joining in at various stages along the way. Since 1998 the final has been decided by a single match at a neutral venue – all finals prior to this were decided over two legs.

No Contest

Sometimes winning a cup can be easier than at others. In 1879 the Vale of Leven were awarded the Scottish Cup Final after Rangers failed to appear for the replay. The first match had finished 1–1 and Rangers had apparently been so upset at having a 'goal' disallowed that they refused to take part in the second match. At the replay the Leven team walked the ball into the unguarded net before being awarded the game.

This strange event may have given the winning side an idea. For just five years later, in 1884, the Cup was awarded to Queen's Park after the non-appearance of their fellow finalists – the Vale of Leven.

Lighting up the Game

Two England internationals, the brothers W. E. and J. C. Clegg, captained teams from the Sheffield area to play an historic match at Bramall Lane, in Sheffield, on 14 October 1878 – this was the first football match played in England under electric lights.

Four wooden towers standing ten metres high were constructed at the corners of the pitch. On each of these four electric lamps were mounted, powered by portable generators. It was a crisp moonlit night and a crowd of approaching 20,000 spectators turned up to watch this evolution that would one day become an integral part of the beautiful game.

Corinthian Men

The formation of the Corinthians, a team consisting of mostly ex–university players, in 1882 was in part a response to the early defeats by Scotland. The new side was intended to build up consistency in the English game and to create a pool of regular players from whom England could draw.

Blowing the Whistle

That essential tool of any football match, the referee's whistle, has a long history. The Acme Thunderer, invented by Birmingham toolmaker Joseph Hudson in 1884, is still used to this day. More than 160 million Thunderers have been made by Hudson & Co, and have been used in 137 countries, in Cup Finals and

World Cups, as well as by policemen and even crewmen on the Titanic.

Rovers' Return

One of the most remarkable sporting feats of the late Chris Balderstone came in September 1975 towards the end of the cricket season, when he dashed from Leicestershire's crucial County Championship match against Derbyshire at Chesterfield to play for Doncaster Rovers in a Fourth Division game against Brentford.

Title-chasing Leicestershire made a disastrous start to their match, posting a score of 77–6 at one stage on the first day. They rallied to achieve a first innings score of 226 all out, before dismissing Derbyshire for 211, with Balderstone returning very tidy bowling figures of one for 13 in nine overs.

Back at the crease for his second innings, Balderstone was 51 not out at close of play. But there was no time to reflect on his day's success. The moment play finished, he sped away in a waiting taxi to pull on his football kit and boots to help Doncaster to a 1–1 home draw with visiting Brentford.

The following morning Balderstone returned to the cricket pitch to continue his innings, completed a century and made 116 runs in total. Leicestershire declared at 260–6. That left Derbyshire with three hours, 20 minutes, to achieve their target of 276. With Balderstone's left-arm spin bowling taking three wickets for 28 runs, the home side were bowled out for 140 with five minutes of the match remaining, and Leicestershire claimed the title.

Scottish Invasion

Before the 1886–7 season Scottish clubs were allowed to compete in the FA Cup. Queen's Park twice reached the final, in 1884 and 1885, losing on both occasions to Blackburn Rovers. Five other Scottish clubs competed during this period as well: Hearts, Partick Thistle, Glasgow Rangers, Renton and Cowlairs.

Giant Killers

Queen's Park Rangers became the first Third Division side to win a major trophy when they beat First Division West Bromwich Albion 3–2 in the 1967 League Cup Final. The feat was even more remarkable as Albion had taken an apparently impregnable 2–0 lead.

Poor Timing

Steve Bloomer, one of English football's earliest superstars, moved to Berlin in July 1914 to become a coach after retiring from playing at the age of 40. But Bloomer, who scored 28 goals in his 23 England games and who was a much-lauded sportsman of his day, got caught up in the outbreak of the First World War only a few weeks after his arrival. He was interned by the German authorities at Ruhleben camp for much of the duration of the hostilities. This however did not dampen his enthusiasm for football and he and other prisoners organized their own football tournaments.

Cash Strapped

Just 15 teams took part in the first FA Cup, and 13 of them were from London. The other two were Donington School from Lincolnshire and, the Scottish team – Queen's Park.

The Scottish team entered the competition at the semi-final stage and were in fact not beaten. They drew 0–0 with Wanderers, but for financial reasons could not remain any longer in England to take part in a replay, so Wanderers went through to the final.

All Aboard

Getting shipwrecked is not something that many footballers have to worry about, but it happened to the Raith Rovers squad in July 1922. Embarking on a tour of the Canary Islands aboard the steamer Highland

Loch, the party was horrified when the ship ran aground off the north-west coast of Spain and the entire crew and all the passengers had to rush for the lifeboats.

Although one of the lifeboats sank, everyone fortunately got off the ship safely. Bravely the Raith squad carried on their tour to the Canaries the next day aboard a P&O ship. And to their enduring credit the Scottish side won all four matches.

French Philosophy

'I feel close to the rebelliousness and vigour of the youth here. Perhaps time will separate us, but nobody can deny that here, behind the windows of Manchester, there is an insane love of football, of celebration and of music.'

Eric Cantona

Double Trouble

Manchester City's Tom Hutchinson had the unenviable distinction of scoring for both sides in the 1981 FA Cup final against Spurs, which ended in a 1–1 draw!

In doing this emulated Bert Turner's feat in the 1947 Cup Final, when he scored for both sides in Charlton's 1–4 defeat by Derby County. Fortunately for Hutchinson, Spurs went on to win the replay and took the Cup in 1981.

Footballer Writers' Association Footballer of the Year

For over half a century members of the Footballer Writers' Association have annually selected the outstanding player of the season in the English game. Inaugurated in 1948, their roll of honour looks like this.

Year	Player	Club
1948	Stanley Matthews	Blackpool
1949	Johnny Carey	Manchester United
1950	Joe Mercer	Arsenal
1951	Harry Johnston	Blackpool
1952	Billy Wright	Wolverhampton Wanderers
1953	Nat Lofthouse	Bolton Wanderers
1954	Tom Finney	Preston North End
1955	Don Revie	Manchester City
1956	Bert Trautmann	Manchester City
1957	Tom Finney	Preston North End
1958	Danny Blanchflower	Tottenham Hotspur
1959	Syd Owen	Luton Town
1960	Bill Slater	Wolverhampton Wanderers
1961	Danny Blanchflower	Tottenham Hotspur
1962	Jimmy Adamson	Burnley
1963	Stanley Matthews	Stoke City
1964	Bobby Moore	West Ham United
1965	Bobby Collins	Leeds United
1966	Bobby Charlton	Manchester United
1967	Jack Charlton	Leeds United
1968	George Best	Manchester United

FOOTBALL

1969	Dave Mackay	Derby County
1969	Tony Book	Manchester City
1970	Billy Bremner	Leeds United
1971	Frank McLintock	Arsenal
1972	Gordon Banks	Stoke City
1973	Pat Jennings	Tottenham Hotspur
1974	Ian Callaghan	Liverpool
1975	Alan Mullery	Fulham
1976	Kevin Keegan	Liverpool
1977	Emlyn Hughes	Liverpool
1978	Kenny Burns	Nottingham Forest
1979	Kenny Dalglish	Liverpool
1980	Terry McDermott	Liverpool
1981	Frans Thijssen	Ipswich Town
1982	Steve Perryman	Tottenham Hotspur
1983	Kenny Dalglish	Liverpool
1984	Ian Rush	Liverpool
1985	Neville Southall	Everton
1986	Gary Lineker	Everton
1987	Clive Allen	Tottenham Hotspur
1988	John Barnes	Liverpool
1989	Steve Nicol	Liverpool
1990	John Barnes	Liverpool
1991	Gordon Strachan	Leeds United
1992	Gary Lineker	Tottenham Hotspur
1993	Chris Waddle	Sheffield Wednesday
1994	Alan Shearer	Blackburn Rovers
1995	Jurgen Klinsmann	Tottenham Hotspur
1996	Eric Cantona	Manchester United

1997	Gianfranco Zola	Chelsea
1998	Dennis Bergkamp	Arsenal
1999	David Ginola	Tottenham Hotspur
2000	Roy Keane	Manchester United
2001	Teddy Sheringham	Manchester United
2002	Robert Pires	Arsenal
2003	Thierry Henry	Arsenal
2004	Thierry Henry	Arsenal
2005	Frank Lampard	Chelsea
2006	Thierry Henry	Arsenal
2007	Cristiano Ronaldo	Manchester United

The Special One

'I intend to give my best, to improve things and to create the football team in relation to my image and my football philosophy.'

José Mourinho

A Farewell to Football

'The admission into the amateur ranks of professional football players is possibly the beginning of the end in an important social movement with which everybody must sympathise. The idea has been to bring together all classes in football and athletics on terms of perfect equality. With the introduction of professionals a new departure is taken. The first effect of the change will be to make the Rugby game the aristocratic one, and the

FOOTBALL

Association game will probably almost die out in the South of England, where it is already declining in favour.'

Manchester Guardian, November 1884

Indoor Football

The first indoor arena used in a World Cup was the Pontiac Silverdome in the US city of Detroit, which was one of the venues for the 1994 World Cup finals.

The Inner Game

Having spent six weeks in a coma, 15-year-old Gareth Knight recovered consciousness after being played a recording of the match between Bolton Wanderers and Reading in the 1995 First Division play-offs. Gareth, a Bolton fan, was revived after hearing his team defeat Reading in a seven-goal thriller, 4–3.

Bosman Ruling

The so-called Bosman ruling, made in 1996 by the European Court of Justice, had a profound effect on the football transfer market. As a result of its implementation players are enabled to move from one club to another at the end of their contract without a transfer fee being paid.

This landmark judgement is named after Belgian player Jean-Marc Bosman, who wished to move to French club Dunkerque from RFC Liege, although the French club did not offer a big enough transfer fee and Liege refused to transfer him. They also dropped him from the first team and reduced his wages, with the result that Bosman took the club to the European Court in Luxembourg and won the right to a free transfer – not only for himself, but every other professional player within the European Union. (Players under 23 may still command a fee, however.)

Backs to the Wall

Football lore holds that the first side to organise a defensive wall at a free-kick was the Northern Ireland side during the World Cup finals in Sweden in 1958, the idea having been the brainchild of Peter Doherty and Danny Blanchflower. Since then every side has organised a wall to try and prevent an attacking team having an easy shot at goal from a free-kick. In order to beat the wall, players will either opt for powering a shot through the wall, or bending the ball around or over it.

The Wake-up Call

In 1953 England's undefeated home record against Continental opposition was shattered by the 'Magic Magyars' – the Hungarian team led by Ferenz Puskas who travelled to Wembley and trounced the home side 6–3. Their victory marked the end of an era in English football, but England were not blind to what had transpired.

'The Hungarians produced some of the finest, most brilliantly applied football it has ever been my privilege to see. The ball did precisely what they wanted ... They were relentless. They were superb.'

Billy Wright, England captain.

'Throughout the game we demonstrated the golden rule of modern football and that is: the good player keeps playing even without the ball. All the time he is placing himself so that when the ball comes to him he is able to make good use of it. We improved the English saying "Kick and run" to "Pass accurately and run into a good position".'

Ferenz Puskas, Hungary captain

'It is easy to lock the stable door after the horse has gone, but I believe the only way to beat this tactical system of the Continentals is by playing the Arsenal type of defensive system ... If the Hungarians or any other team have the ball in midfield, let them have it. They have got to get to our penalty area to score goals, because that is where the goal is, and to win matches goals have to be scored ... I believe that if our team, attack and defence, retreat to our eighteen-yard line and let the Hungarians come to us, we are compact and as soon as their attack is 'broken down', then is the time for us to assume the attack (defenders and attackers together) using the square ball and then the through one, which the Continentals are now doing.'

From Soccer the Lawton Way, Tommy Lawton

Directory Enquiries

In order to safeguard a football pool worth the equivalent of £1000, an Italian punter placed I inside his local Turin telephone directory. Unluckily for him, while he was away from home, the telephone company called to take away his old directory and replace it with the new edition. This left the expectant punter with the unenviable task of searching through something in the region of 235,000 pages of discarded directories.

Away Goals Rule

In European competition and two-legged League Cup ties, any goal scored by an away side is counted as double in the event of an aggregate draw. Thus, if a team won their home match 1–0 but lost the away tie 2–1, they would progress into the next round on away goals. In European competition, this rule is invoked at the end of the second 90 minutes, in the League Cup at the end of extra time.

FOOTBALL

England Goals

Peter Crouch heads the list of leading England goal scorers in a calendar year and he is in good company as this list shows.

11 goals
Peter Crouch 2006

9 goals
Stan Mortensen 1947
Tommy Lawton 1947
Nat Lofthouse 1952
Jimmy Greaves 1960
Gary Lineker 1987 and 1991

8 goals
Jimmy Greaves 1963
Gary Lineker 1986, 1990
Alan Shearer 1996

7 goals
Tommy Taylor 1957
Geoff Hurst 1966
Roger Hunt 1966, 1969
Martin Chivers 1971
Michael Owen 2005

You'll Never Walk Alone

Paula O'Sullivan might have cause to be less than enthusiastic about Liverpool's FA Cup victory in 1965. She was christened soon afterwards and given the names of the winning team, so that her birth certificate read: Paula St John Lawrence Lawler Byrne Strong Yates Stevenson Callaghan Hunt Milne Smith Thompson Shankley Bennett Paisley O'Sullivan. Her father was a die-hard Liverpool supporter, so much so that he overlooked minor details like the correct spelling of the name of the captain (Yeats) and the manager (Shankly).

Re-writing the Corner Rules

During a match between Everton and Arsenal in the 1924–5 football season the Everton right-wing, Sam Chedgzoy was instrumental in bringing about a rapid revision of the football rule book.

That afternoon Everton were playing at home against Arsenal and before the match a local Liverpool sports reporter asked Chedgzoy to try an experiment that he hoped would point up a flaw in the laws of the game as they then were. Aided by a payment of £2, the reporter persuaded the Everton wing to try an experiment if he had the chance to take a corner; his opportunity came in the first half.

With Arsenal and Everton players gathered in front of the goal waiting for the usual lofted ball from the corner flag, Chedgzoy took them all completely by surprise when he dribbled the ball himself into the penalty area and thumped it through the Arsenal defence, past the astonished goalkeeper and into the back of the net.

The referee refused to allow the goal, despite Chedgzoy's protestations that there was nothing stated in the rules to prevent him from doing what he had done. Everton went on to lose 3–2, but the referee had been wrong not to allow the goal to stand: at the time the rules said nothing about corner-takers being allowed just one touch of the ball. Within 48 hours, though, this anomaly had been rectified and the Liverpool sports reporter presumably had the satisfaction of seeing his £2 put to lasting use in the interests of the game.

Roman Holiday

The Italians are well known for their passion for football, and it may be that the sport has been in their blood for a long time. There are ancient reports which suggest that a Roman team played an early version of football against an English village side in 217AD. The English side apparently won – though what happened about an away leg is not recorded.

By George

The Newcastle and Arsenal inside forward, George Eastham, established two memorable milestones in football history during his career; indeed he might well have added a third by virtue of being a member of the England squad in the 1966 World Cup, but he never made the team sheet during that historic competition, which saw the home nation lift the trophy.

Eastham's first milestone came in 1960 after he applied to Newcastle, to whom he was contracted as a player, seeking a transfer. Under the old 'retain and transfer' system this request was denied, with Newcastle holding on to Eastham's registration in order to block his move elsewhere.

Aided by the Professional Footballer's Association, George Eastham took Newcastle to court and won. The landmark ruling in his favour allowed players to move clubs for free once they had completed their contracts, giving them a say in their careers which they had never enjoyed before. The PFA also succeeded in making a major improvement in player's wages when they succeeded in overturning the limit that had set a maximum wage for players, with the result that Johnny Haynes immediately became the first £100 player at Fulham.

In 1960 George Eastham moved to Arsenal and three

years later set in place his second notable milestone, when he played for England against Brazil and so became the first son to follow his father onto the football pitch to play for his country; his father, George 'Diddler' Eastham had played for England in 1935.

So far that achievement has only been repeated twice: by Brian and Nigel Clough and the Lampards, Frank senior and Frank junior.

Continental Divide

The governing body of world football, the Fédération Internationale de Football Association (FIFA), was founded at the rear of the HQ of the Union Française de Sports Athlétiques in Paris, on 21 May 1904. This helps to explain why the name of the organization is French. The countries whose representatives signed the original document were: France, Belgium, Denmark, Holland, Spain, Sweden and Switzerland. The English Football Association the oldest in the world refused to join until April 1905 and even after that had an uneasy relationship with FIFA for many years.

Golden Boy

'Wayne Rooney is the golden boy of English football. Don't kill him because you will need him.'

Sven-Goran Eriksson

Football Transfer Milestones

Year	Player	Transfer from	Transfer to
1905	Alf Common (England) Fee £1k	Sunderland (England)	Middlesbrough (England)
1929	David Jack (England) Fee £10k	Bolton Wdrs (England)	Arsenal (England)
1932	Bernabe Ferreyra (Argentina) Fee £23k	Tigre (Argentina)	River Plate (Argentina)
1952	Hans Jepson (Sweden) Fee £52k	Amateur	Napoli (Italy)
1954	Juan Schiaffino (Uruguay) Fee £72k	Penarol (Uruguay)	AC Milan (Italy)
1957	Enrique Omar Sivori (Argentina) Fee £93k	River Plate (Argentina)	Juventus (Italy)
1961	Luis Suarez (Spain) Fee £142k	Barcelona (Spain)	Inter Milan (Italy)
1963	Angelo Sormani (Brazil) Fee £250k	Mantova (Italy)	AS Roma (Italy)

FOOTBALL

1968	Pietro Anastasi (Italy) Fee £500k	Varese (Italy)	Juventus (Italy)
1973	Johan Cruyff (Holland) Fee £922k	Ajax Amsterdam (Holland)	Barcelona (Spain)
1975	Giuseppe Savoldi (Italy) Fee £1.2m	Bologna (Italy)	Napoli (Italy)
1978	Paolo Rossi (Italy) Fee £1.75m	Juventus (Italy)	Vicenza (Italy)
1982	Diego Maradona (Argentina) Fee £3m	Boca Juniors (Argentina)	Barcelona (Spain)
1984	Diego Maradona (Argentina) Fee £5m	Barcelona (Spain)	Napoli (Italy)
1987	Ruud Gullit (Holland) Fee £6m	PSV Eindhoven (Holland)	AC Milan (Italy)
1990	Roberto Baggio (Italy) Fee £8m	Fiorentina (Italy)	Juventus (Italy)
1992	Jean Pierre Papin (France) Fee £10m	Marseille (France)	AC Milan (Italy)

1992	Gianluca Vialli (Italy) Fee £12m	Sampdoria (Italy)	Juventus (Italy)
1996	Alan Shearer (England) Fee £15m	Blackburn Rovers (England)	Newcastle Utd (England)
1997	Ronaldo (Brazil) Fee £18m	Barcelona (Spain)	Inter Milan (Italy)
1998	Denilson (Brazil) Fee £32m	Sao Paulo (Brazil)	Inter Milan (Italy)
2000	Hernan Crespo (Argentina) Fee £35.5m	Parma (Italy)	Lazio (Italy)
2000	Luis Figo (Portugal) Fee £37m	Barcelona (Spain)	Real Madrid (Spain)
2005	Zinedine Zidane (Italy) Fee £45.6m	Juventus (Italy)	Real Madrid (Spain)

Re-Writing the Rule Book

In the years of the 20th century that pre-dated the outbreak of the First World War some significant changes were made to the rules of football. The penalty area which had previously stretched the full width of the pitch was reduced in size. After the award by the referee of a free kick or a corner players against whom the kick had been awarded were required to retreat ten yards before the kick was taken. Goalkeepers who had previously been allowed to handle the ball anywhere on the pitch were now restricted to only handling the ball in the penalty area.

By the end of the 1924–5 season football had become very defensive and many games became stop-start affairs with numerous free kicks, brought about by the offside traps which many teams had perfected. The offside rule as it stood required three opposing players to be between an attacking player and the goal when the ball was played. The number of offside decisions arising from this led to a significant change in the offside rule, which was implemented from the start of the 1925–6 season. This reduced the number of defenders that had to be between the goal from the most advanced attacking player, for him to be onside, from three to two and it had an immediate effect in livening up matches everywhere. In the first season under the new rules over 1,600 more League goals were scored.

Substitute player were allowed in the English League from the start of the 1965–6 season provided that they were replacing a player who had sustained an injury. However, the injury requirement was dropped when it became clear that players were feigning injury in order to allow a substitute to be sent on.

Goalkeepers faced further limitations on their play in 1967–8 when the rules were changed to limit them to taking only four steps with the ball before releasing it.

Railway Dispute

The 1901 FA Cup Final between Tottenham Hotspur and Sheffield United went to a replay at Bolton. However, the attendance was only 20,470, the smallest crowd to watch an FA Cup final in the entire 20th century. This was not due to any lack of interest on the part of supporters. It came about because the railway authorities refused cheap excursion tickets, as Bolton railway station was being rebuilt.

Bobby Moore: Goalkeeper

The semi-final played on 26 January 1972 between Stoke City and West Ham United in the League Cup competition will probably be best remembered as the game when Bobby Moore, playing in goal, almost saved a penalty. The tie had started on 8 December 1971 at Stoke, when West Ham had won 2–1. The second leg at Upton Park saw Stoke pull back that goal and the first play-off had resulted in a goal-less draw at Hillsborough.

FOOTBALL

The fourth match had been running 13 minutes when Stoke's Terry Conroy collided with West Ham's goalkeeper, Bobby Ferguson, and manager Ron Greenwood decided that Moore should deputise in goal. Then West Ham's full-back, John McDowell, conceded a penalty. Bernard kick from the penalty spot, Moore smothered the shot but was unable to hold on to the ball and Bernard put it in the net on the rebound.

West Ham responded by scoring twice and Ferguson returned to the pitch to resume his goalkeeping duties. Dobing then equalised for Stoke and Terry Conroy clinched their place in the final with the goal that gave them a 3–2 victory.

Spreading the Joy

'This tour takes the rarely seen trophy – the jewel in the crown of world football – to fans around the world, with the aim of spreading happiness and hope to make the world a better place.'

Sepp Blatter

Disorderly Conduct

Referee Alejandro Otero didn't limit himself to yellow or even red cards when a Libertadores Cup match between Boca Juniors and Peru's Sporting Cristal got out of hand in Buenos Aires on 15 March 1971. As a mass brawl broke out, Señor Otero called in the police, who arrested 19 players. Three had to go to hospital for treatment, the remainder to the police station. All were given a 30-day prison sentence for disorderly conduct, though this was later reduced to suspended sentences. Back home in Peru, government officials said the Cristal team had defended themselves with 'honour and nobility'.

An English Disease?

'Unlike the Brazilians we start looking for faults as soon as we recognize a player's skill. I've had it pushed down my throat ever since I was a kid. Of course the runners and tacklers are part of the game, but people don't have a go at them if they can't play forty-yard balls or go past three men at a time. They don't expect them to do things skilful players are good at. . .That is the way we are in England and maybe it's part of the reason Brazil do it a bit more than us at international level.'

Glenn Hoddle

Beating the Age Barrier

When Billy Meredith played for Manchester City against Newcastle United in an FA Cup semi-final on 29 March 1924, at 49 years eight months, he became the oldest player ever to appear in the FA Cup competition proper.

FOOTBALL

Meredith was also the oldest player to play in a home international when, at almost 46, he played for Wales against England on 15 March 1920.

Strip Changes

Manchester United have not always played in their traditional red and white strip. In their previous existence as Newton Heath the club played in green and gold and then white and blue. Even after switching to red shirts and white shorts in 1902 they haven't always kept the same main strip. For five years from 1922 United wore white shirts with a large red 'V' on them and for one season in 1934 they sported maroon and white.

Double Hat-tricks

The World Cup match between Brazil and Poland, which was played in Strasbourg on 5 June 1938, saw a remarkable feat of scoring. Brazil's Léonidas da Silva scored a hat-trick on the 18th, 25th and 44th minutes, followed by a fourth in the 93rd minute. In reply, Poland's Ernst Willimowski hit a hat-trick of his own on the 22nd, 59th and 88th minutes, followed by a fourth in the 107th minute. The match was finally secured in extra time when Romeo blasted in the winner for Brazil.

Sharp Shooting

Seconds after the kick-off in a memorable match between Corinthians and Rio Preto at Brazil's Bahia stadium, the ball was passed to Roberto Rivelino who blasted a shot goalwards from the halfway line and watch it sail unopposed into the net for a blistering opening goal.

It appeared that Rivelino's focus on the match was somewhat ahead of that of Isadore Irandir, the Rip Preto goalkeeper, who was still completing his pre-match prayers in his goalmouth when Rivelino's shot whistled past his ear.

With family pride at stake, the goalkeeper's brother, Joachim, ran onto the pitch before play resumed, pulled out a revolver and emptied six shots into the ball. As he was led away the crowd greeted him with a good-natured ovation.

Seeing Red

The rivalry between Manchester City and Manchester United has always been intense. But at the start of the 20th century there was a very strange mass exodus of City stars to United thanks to a major football scandal of the day.

FOOTBALL

At that time professional players were supposed to be on a fixed wage of £4 per game. But the authorities discovered in 1905 that City had been playing its star players £6, or even £7 a match. As a result, five City directors were dismissed and some 17 players were banned from ever pulling on a City shirt again. Local rivals United were not slow in taking advantage of their neighbour's misfortunes.

The Reds quickly snapped up some of the City stars, including the great Billy Meredith, who all moved their skills to United – and after serving a ban made their debuts in January 1907. Billy Meredith ended up playing a large number of games for both Manchester clubs, chalking up 303 appearances for United and 366 for City.

Hall of Fame – Male Players

The Hall of Fame was created at the National Football Museum in Preston in 2002, when 29 people who were deemed to have made an 'outstanding and lasting contribution to English football' became the first names on its 'roll of honour'. Each year a selection panel of major personalities in the game, among them Sir Bobby Charlton, Sir Alex Ferguson, Sir Bobby Robson, Brian Cough and Mark Lawrenson, nominate ten new members from the categories of male players, female players and managers, who are inducted at a prestigious charity awards ceremony.

To date male players inducted to the Hall of Fame are as follows.

> Tony Adams
> Viv Anderson
> Alan Ball
> Gordon Banks
> John Barnes
> Colin Bell
> George Best
> Danny Blanchflower
> Liam Brady
> Billy Bremner
> Eric Cantona
> John Charles
> Jack Charlton
> Sir Bobby Charlton
> Kenny Dalglish
> Dixie Dean
> Peter Doherty
> Duncan Edwards
> Sir Tom Finney
> Paul Gascoigne
> Ryan Giggs
> Jimmy Greaves
> Alan Hansen

FOOTBALL

Johnny Haynes
Roger Hunt
Sir Geoff Hurst
Alex James
Pat Jennings
Roy Keane
Kevin Keegan
Dennis Law
Tommy Lawton
Gary Lineker
Nat Lofthouse
Dave Mackay
Wilf Mannion
Sir Stanley Matthews
Jackie Milburn
Bobby Moore
Stan Mortensen
Martin Peters
Bryan Robson
Ian Rush
Peter Schmeichel
Alan Shearer
Peter Shilton
Bert Trautmann
Arthur Wharton
Billy Wright
Ian Wright
Gianfranco Zola

Taming the Terraces

'Don't think because you are on the stand you have a right to shout instructions at the players. They know what to do without any assistance from you.

Don't snap your neighbour's nose off because he thinks differently from you. You have come to see your side win, and he has perhaps come to see the other.

Don't make a nuisance of yourself to those around you by continually bellowing at the top of your voice, it gets on people's nerves and takes away a lot of the enjoyment of the game, besides making yourself look ridiculous.'

From a Sheffield United programme, October 1907

Going Dutch

Blackpool first donned their distinctive tangerine strip in the 1923–24 season, and their first match with it was a 2–2 draw with Oldham Athletic. It seems the colour had been suggested by a director of the club, Albert Hargreaves, who had refereed an international game involving Holland. He apparently thought that orange – the colour the Dutch team still wears – would help Blackpool stand out among fellow English clubs.

FOOTBALL

League Managers Association Code of Conduct

1. A Manager shall strictly observe the terms of his contract with his Club and shall not (either by himself or through any third party) enter into negotiations with another Club relating to his employment without having first obtained the permission of his Club to do so.

2. A Manager shall not take any steps (including the making of statements to the media) to induce or which are intended to induce any Player or other employee employed by another Club to act in breach of the terms of his contract with that other Club.

3. A Manager shall comply with the Laws of the Game and the Rules of The Football Association, the Rules of The FA Premier League, the rules of any competition in which his Club participates and his Club Rules and he shall not encourage or invite and person (including Players and other employees of his Club) to act in breach of the same but shall take all possible steps to ensure that they comply with them.

4. A Manager shall use his best endeavours to ensure that there is in force at his Club a fair and effective disciplinary policy applicable to Players and other

employees under his control and that it is applied consistently.

5. A Manager shall take all reasonable steps to ensure that Players and other employees under his control accept and observe the authority and decisions of match officials.

6. A Manager shall not make public and unfair criticism of any match official or any other Manager or any Player, Official or employee of his or another Club.

7. A Manager shall conduct himself at all times in an ethical and professional manner and shall observe the highest standards of integrity and fair dealing.

8. A Manager shall take all possible steps to promote the reputation of the game of Association Football and to prevent it being brought into disrepute.

Added Incentive

When Fulham lined up against Bristol Rovers in the FA Cup fourth round tie, the Fulham players may have had more than victory on their minds. Tommy Trinder, who was a director of the club, had offered to give his overcoat to any Fulham player who scored a hat-trick When Arthur Stevens sent his third goal of the match into the Bristol Rovers goal, Trinder could be seen reaching over the balcony at Craven Cottage waving his coat. His enthusiasm did not escape the attention of the FA who 'suspected that an illegal payment may have been made.'

Drop Ball

Until the 1980s, a match was restarted after players had been injured by the referee dropping the ball between two players, one from each side. Since neither player could touch the ball until it had hit the ground, a melee usually resulted, the object being to kick the ball to a team mate. Now it is usual for the referee to indicate that one player should kick the ball back to the opposing goalkeeper to restore possession.

Symbolic Presidency

'I think it is a happy coincidence that the ball is the instrument of the sport represented by FIFA. It is round without angles or sharp edges. Without its unlimited surface, lines may criss-cross to infinity. When in motion it can be impelled in all directions with no deformation and without losing its characteristics, to fulfil its performance it is necessary never to be still, always on the move. I feel you can take it as a symbol of my work as your president of FIFA.'

Joao Havelange

By the Book

10 19th-century Landmarks in the Development of Football

1848 The first code of Football Rules was drawn up at Cambridge University.

1863 Carrying the ball was outlawed (anyone who wanted to carry on played rugby).

1869 Goal kicks were introduced.

1870 11 players a-side became the standard number in a football team.

1872 Corner kicks were introduced.

1873 Free kicks were introduced.

1874 Umpires were introduced to officiate football matches.

1875 Crossbars replaced tapes between goal posts.

1882 Two-handed throw-ins became mandatory, to prevent players throwing-in the ball one-handed.

1891 Penalties were introduced.

Wolverhampton Who?

Wolverhampton Sunday League side Oxbarn Social Club arranged a friendly match in Germany in 1973 and looked forward to mixing a little gentle football with a pleasant Continental break.

This innocent plan began to take an unexpected turn soon after the Oxbarn party arrived at their destination and entered their opponents' ground, so markedly different to the ones they were used to playing on back home. SVW Mainz, who played in the German first division, were looking forward to taking on their visitors from Wolverhampton, since Wolverhampton Wanderers were one of the foremost football teams in Britain at that time.

As the Oxbarn Club secretary disarmingly explained afterwards, 'I thought it looked posh, and when I heard the other side were on an £80 bonus to win, I said to myself, "Something is wrong."' His private reflection proved to be all too accurate. Somewhere in the correspondence any reference to Sunday League, or indeed his club's actual name had been overlooked.

When Mainz scored their 15th goal, the Oxbarn goalkeeper appeared to fall on his knees, as if imploring the heavens for the final whistle. His prayers were answered almost immediately – by goals 16 and 17.

'They behaved very well,' commented the Oxbarn secretary of the home fans. 'Whenever we got the ball, they gave a prolonged cheer.'

Sadly even this touch of local support was not enough to save Oxbarn Social from losing 21–0.

Hall of Fame – Female Players

Since its inauguration, in 2002, at the National Football Museum in Preston, the following outstanding footballers have been inducted in the category of female players.

> Debbie Bampton
> Gillian Coultard
> Sue Lopez
> Lily Parr
> Hope Powell

Forget-me-nots

Every player's worst nightmare came true for Stan Richards when he arrived for his debut international for Wales, against England at Maine Road, Manchester, in 1946. He had forgotten his boots.

It wasn't just his debut, though – it turned out to be his only match for Wales.

Guest Appearance

Partick Thistle hosted a European Cup match in November 1955 – though unfortunately they were not playing in the competition themselves. Hibernian were unable to play their 'away' leg against Djurgaarden because of severe winter in Sweden, so the European Cup tie was played at Partick's Firhill ground. Hibs won both legs.

The Chelsea Challenge

'Roman Abramovich has parked his Russian tanks on our lawn and is firing £50 notes at us.'

David Dein, Arsenal vice-chairman

Slow Starter

Bob Crompton, who made his debut for England at right-back in 1902 and who won 41 caps in all, had been a reluctant footballer to start with. Crompton preferred water polo and swimming as a young man and it took Blackburn Rovers months to persuade him to join them, after they spotted him playing in a Sunday league. He once caused something of a sensation when in 1907 he turned up at Ewood Park in a car – a rare luxury in those days.

Senior Player

Manchester United player Billy Meredith became the oldest person to play international soccer for Wales when he took to the field against England on 15 March 1920 at Highbury. He was aged 45 years and 229 days. To add to his pleasure Wales won the game 2–1.

Meredith was selected for Wales 71 times up to 1920 but only collected 51 caps because the various clubs he played for refused to release him for the other games.

Viva Vava!

One of the Brazilian heroes of the 1958 World Cup finals was their striker Vava (real name Edvaldo Izidio Neto). However, his popularity with his team mates was almost his undoing. After scoring his second goal against the Soviet Union in a pool match, Vava was so enthusiastically mobbed by fellow players that he was left unconscious on the ground and needed medical treatment. Fortunately for Brazil, he was all right to play in the final, scoring once as Brazil beat hosts Sweden 5–2.

On the Airwaves

On St George's Day (23 April) 1927, the first radio commentary of a football match was broadcast in the UK. The commentator on the Arsenal–Cardiff City game was George Allinson, who undertook the task despite being an Arsenal director. His assistant that afternoon was Derek McCulloch, who went on to achieve radio fame of his own as 'Uncle Mac', the presenter of Children's Hour.

FOOTBALL

Victory from the Jaws of Defeat

Despite a defeat in the second round of the 1971–2 European Cup Winners' Cup, Glasgow Rangers still managed to lift the trophy. This seemingly unlikely event came about following their tie against Sporting Lisbon. On 20 October Rangers won the home leg 3–2, but lost the away leg in Portugal on 3 November 4–3.

They should have progressed to the next round on the away-goals rule, but the referee demanded a penalty shoot-out in which three Rangers players had their shots saved and a fourth missed the target, handing Sporting a 2–0 win.

However, the match official was later suspended and the tie was awarded to Rangers, after the away-goals rule had finally, and correctly, been invoked.

Utility Player

One of the more versatile players in soccer history was Johnny Carey. Between 1937 and 1953 he played in every position except outside-left (and that includes goalkeeper) for Manchester United and also filled six different spots for the Republic of Ireland and Northern Ireland teams.

Hall of Fame – Managers

Since its inauguration, in 2002, at the National Football Museum in Preston, the following legendary managers have been inducted.

> Sir Matt Busby
> Herbert Chapman
> Brian Clough
> Stan Cullis
> Sir Alex Ferguson
> Dario Gradi
> Ron Greenwood
> Howard Kendall
> Bill Nicholson
> Bob Paisley
> Sir Alf Ramsey
> Don Revie
> Sir Bobby Robson
> Bill Shankly
> Arsene Wenger
> Walter Winterbottom

> Special Category – Ambassador of Football
> FIFA President Joseph S. Blatter

Winning Odds

When English football was subject to a maximum wage payable to players, it was rumoured that a number of games were the subject of match-fixing, whereby one side would win in order to finish high enough up the League in order to earn their players additional bonuses.

With the scrapping of the maximum wage these rumours diminished, but in 1964 the English game was rocked by its biggest-ever scandal when three Sheffield Wednesday players – Tony Kay, Peter Swann and David 'Bronco' Layne, were accused and subsequently found guilty of fixing the result of their match against Ipswich Town on 1 December 1962. There was no suggestion any Ipswich players were involved; the Wednesday players were only able to influence how many goals their side conceded as part of a fixed-odds betting coup. All three were banned from playing football for life and were sentenced to four months in prison. Tony Kay had previously become Britain's most expensive footballer, when he had transferred from Sheffield to Everton, and both he and Peter Swann were England internationals. Their life bans were later reduced to eight years

Fairs Fair

The Inter-Cities Fairs Cup was introduced to the football calendar in 1955, the same year the European Cup was introduced. Initially invitations were extended to those cities that staged trade fairs, and a composite London side reached the first final in 1958 (the inaugural competition having taken three years to complete) before being beaten 8–2 on aggregate by Barcelona. The competition, now annual, ran until the 1970–71 season when it was replaced by the UEFA Cup.

Hands Off

In 1992 FIFA changed the rule so that a goalkeeper could not pick the ball up from a pass back to him by one of his outfield players. This became punishable by an indirect free-kick at the spot where the goalkeeper picked up the ball, although the rule change allowed a pass to be headed or chested back without penalty.

Saved by the Whistle

The referee's final whistle can seldom have been so important as it was at the end of the FA Cup semi-final game between Sheffield Wednesday and Huddersfield Town on 22 March 1930. Just as the whistle was blown, a shot from Wednesday's Jack Allen was on its way into the Huddersfield net. But the referee refused to allow the goal on the grounds that the ball had not crossed the goal line when he began to blow the whistle for full-time, and Huddersfield went on to clinch the final with a 2–1 win.

FOOTBALL

Jack Allen received some compensation two years later when he played for Newcastle in the final and scored two goals to make them champions that year.

Early Promise

Manchester United's 10–1 defeat of Wolverhampton Wanderers in the 1892–93 season was their first-ever League win (they were still called Newton Heath at the time) in only their seventh League match. Six players scored in all. But, amazingly, they still finished bottom of the division that year.

United went even further in March 1895 when they beat Walsall by the staggering score of 14–0. But Walsall cannily complained about the state of the pitch – and the result did not stand.

Doing a Treble in Europe

During his playing career in the 1950s and 1960s, Gordon Smith held the unique distinction among Scottish players of having played in the European Cup for three different Scottish clubs, none of which were either Celtic or Rangers.

For the record, Smith played for: Dundee, Heart of Midlothian and Hibernian.

England's Most Capped Players

As of the summer of 2007 England's ten most capped players were the following.

Name	Caps
Peter Shilton	125
Bobby Moore	108
Bobby Charlton	106
Billy Wright	105
David Beckham	96
Bryan Robson	90
Kenny Sansom	86
Gary Neville	85
Ray Wilkins	84
Michael Owen	82

Two's Company

The Liechtenstein Cup Final became a familiar affair from 1946, when sides FC Triesen and FC Vaduz contested it on nine consecutive occasions.

Charity Shield

In 1908 the Football Association set up a charity shield for an annual match between two teams selected by the Association, with the proceeds to go to charity. The first of these matches was played that year at Stamford

FOOTBALL

Bridge when the League champions, Manchester United, beat the Southern League champions, Queen's Park Rangers, 4–0 after previously drawing 1–1. That was the only time that a Shield match has been replayed.

From 1974 the Shield match was played at Wembley as a curtain-raiser to the forthcoming season, with the reigning League champions playing the current FA Cup holders.

Brazilian Derby Games

One of the great rivalries in world football is between the two Rio de Janeiro clubs Flamengo and Fluminense. One of these so-called 'Flu–Fla' derbies at the Maracana stadium in 1963 attracted a massive crowd of 177,656 people.

Winning Both Ways

The striker Frank Stapleton won two FA Cup winners' medals with Manchester United in 1983 and 1985 as well as one against them – for Arsenal in 1979.

Stan Crowther also played for and against Manchester United in an FA Cup final – for Aston Villa in 1957 and for United a year later. Crowther in fact played for both Villa and United in the FA Cup in the same year;

he had moved to United from Aston Villa just before the Manchester club's fifth-round tie with Sheffield Wednesday. Normally, a player who moves in a season having played in the Cup for one team is 'cup-tied' and can't play for another team in the same competition. But the rules were understandably relaxed for United because of the Munich air disaster of that year in which so many of their players had been killed or injured.

Goal Drought

Some players have very lean patches when it comes to scoring goals. Consider Shay Brennan who scored twice on his Manchester United debut in 1958, but managed only another four goals in total in a further 355 games for the club.

Gre-No-Li

This was the nickname given to the famous Swedish forward line of the 1940s. 'Gre-No-Li' was derived from the combining the beginning of the surnames of a trio of outstanding players: Gunnar Gren, Gunnar Nordahl, and Nils Liedholm. The three helped Sweden to the Olympic gold medal and were then snapped up as a group by Italian club Milan, whom they helped to win four titles in the 1950s, after 40 years with no silverware in the club's cabinet.

FOOTBALL

Gunnar Nordahl distinguished himself further as the club's all-time top scorer with 210 goals and a season's record of 35 goals, which he scored in 1949–50.

England's Leading Goal Scorers

As of the summer of 2007 the following were England's highest scoring players.

Name	Goals
Bobby Charlton	49
Gary Lineker	48
Jimmy Greaves	44
Michael Owen	37
Tom Finney	30
Nat Lofthouse	30
Alan Shearer	30
Vivian Woodward	29
Stephen Bloomer	28
David Platt	27

England Managers

In 1946 England went down 1–0 to Switzerland in Zurich and the FA concluded that the time had come to dispense with the old system of inviting guest trainers to prepare the team for international competition in favour of a permanent manager. Stanley Rous, secretary of the Football Association at the time, promoted chief coach Walter Winterbottom to become the first England manager proper. Winterbottom and his team responded emphatically during their end of season tour in Portugal, when they thrashed the home side 10–0 with the first goal coming just 20 seconds after kick-off.

What, one wonders, would many of Winterbottom's successors below, have given for an England score line like that, especially one achieved against a footballing nation with the prowess of England's Portuguese opponents that day?

Manager	Period in charge
Walter Winterbottom	1946–63
Alf Ramsey	1963–74
Joe Mercer	1974
Don Revie	1974–77
Ron Greenwood	1977–82
Bobby Robson	1982–90
Graham Taylor	1990–93
Terry Venables	1994–96
Glenn Hoddle	1996–99
Howard Wilkinson	1999 (one match)
Kevin Keegan	1999–2000
Howard Wilkinson	2000 (one match)
Peter Taylor	2000 (one match)
Sven-Goran Eriksson	2001–06
Steve McClaren	2006–

FOOTBALL

Zimmer Lout

At 82, Sam Phillips was not the usual suspect for a bout of football hooliganism. Even so, he found himself banned from Ledbury Town's home games during the 1980–1 season.

His offence? Apparently he had attacked a referee leaving his shirt 'torn beyond repair'. During his ban, Mr Phillips watched the Herefordshire team's home matches through a hole in a hedge.

Rapid Fire

Bryan Robson's goal scored against France 27 seconds after kick-off at Bilbao on 16 June 1982 stands as the fastest goal scored by an England player on international duty. Not far behind come Gareth Southgate's 36th-second goal against South Africa which he scored in Durban on 22 May 2003; Bryan Robson (again) with a netted strike in 38 seconds against Yugoslavia on 13 December 1989 – that was also the quickest England goal scored at Wembley; and Gary Lineker's opening goal against Malaysia, which found the net 42 seconds after kick-off in Kuala Lumpur on 12 June, 1991, when England took on home side Malaysia.

Teddy Sheringham can claim to have bettered all of these in terms of personal performance when he was sent on as an England substitute against Greece at Old Trafford on 6 October 2001 and had the ball in the Greek net ten seconds later.

However, Willie Hall still heads the field with his performance against Northern Ireland on 16 November, 1938, once again at Old Trafford, when he scored an England hat-trick in three and a half minutes.

A Cup Run to Remember

In the 1932–3 FA Cup competition Brighton & Hove Albion failed to apply from exemption from the qualifying rounds and consequently found themselves scoring nearly 30 goals in their first three games.

Brighton's tally went like this. They opened their campaign with a 12–0 win over Shoreham, moved on to Worthing whom they defeated 7–1. Next up were Hastings, who were despatched 9–0, followed by Barnet, who were beaten 4–0, and Crystal Palace, who restricted Brighton to a single-goal margin in their 2–1 victory. Wrexham did the same, though Brighton went through 3-2, before they came up against Chelsea. Yet even they fell to Brighton, who had the ball in the Chelsea net for their first goal in less than 30 seconds from kick-off. The London side pulled one back, but this was not enough to stop Brighton progressing to the fourth round, when they beat Bradford Park Avenue 2–1.

FOOTBALL

It was when they reached the fifth round that Brighton's momentum ran out. West Ham held them to a 2-2 draw and then went on to win the replay 1-0. Having scored a total of 43 goals, Brighton's Cup run came to an end for that year.

Short Measure

After Arbroath had scored a famous 4-3 victory over Rangers in 1884 in the Scottish Cup, Rangers lodged a complaint about the size of the pitch. Sure enough, upon measurement, the ground's width was found to be several inches short of the required distance. So the game had to be replayed – and Rangers put eight goals past Arbroath.

A Numbers Game

English players wore numbered shirts for the first time in the FA Cup Final of the 1932-3 season. Everton, who won 3-0, wore shirts numbered from 1 (the goalkeeper) to 11. Their opponents, Manchester City, were numbered from 12 to 22 (their goalkeeper).

Paying Over the Odds

In 1887 disgruntled opponents called in a private detective to investigate Hibernian, who had just won the Scottish Cup. The detective discovered that Hibs had been paying one player, a stone mason, more for missing three days work than he was usually paid by his employer in a week. At the time so-called 'broken time' payments, that is compensation for loss of earnings at work, were allowed – but not being paid to play.

Not Playing the Game

The England centre-forward of the 1890s G. O. Smith had an unusual quirk for a player in his position – he refused to head the ball. He believed that the ball should stay on the ground and that any side whose forwards needed to use their head were not playing the game correctly. Smith was the first England centre-forward to reach 20 caps, scoring 11 goals along the way so maybe he had a point.

Playing to the Whistle

Referees can win and lose matches – and sometimes in very heated circumstances. At the 1930 World Cup finals in Uruguay, France were playing Argentina in an opening Group One pool match on 15 July with the South American side leading 1–0. A French player seemed on the verge of scoring when the Brazilian referee blew his whistle – six minutes early. After a period of pandemonium the mistake was realised and the game restarted – but France never came close again to scoring. It was Argentina and not France who went through to the semi-finals.

FOOTBALL

Tragic Result

One of the first major disasters at a football match was on 5 April 1902 during a Scotland-England match at Ibrox in Glasgow. Part of a stand collapsed just a few minutes into the game killing 25 people and injuring many more. The game in fact continued because the authorities were unaware of the full seriousness of the incident and anyway didn't want to cause more panic by stopping play.

The match, which ended 1–1, was later replayed in Birmingham when the score was 2–2. The original Ibrox fixture is now generally regarded as an unofficial or friendly match. All the gate receipts from the second match went towards the disaster fund set up for the victims of the tragedy.

Up the Avenue

Trevor Bailey has a deserved reputation as a fine cricketer, an all-rounder who played for both Essex and England. But he was also a fine footballer. He was part of the amateur side Walthamstow Avenue that held Manchester United to a 1–1 draw in an FA Cup tie at Old Trafford on 31 January 1953.

Manchester United had taken the title the previous season, demolishing Arsenal 6–1 on the last day of season, and were just three points adrift of that season's Division 1's leaders, West Bromwich Albion. Alas for the Avenue, they fared less well in the replay at Highbury – losing 5–2 – although they did have the satisfaction of playing in front of 53,000 people, who had turned up to see whether the minnows from the Isthmian League could pull something out for the bag and beat the side that had trounced Arsenal so comprehensively less than a year before.

Suspended for the Duration

When Football League matches were suspended at the outbreak of the Second World War, Middlesbrough had finished bottom of Division I in the previous season. However, they waited another eight seasons before finally being relegated.

The story was less happy for Blackpool, the League leaders that season. They never reached that pinnacle again; their best position being runners-up, 11 points behind Manchester United, in 1956.

United We Stand

There are 20 top-flight British football clubs that have the word United in their name. They are listed here in the chronological order in which they became 'United'.

FOOTBALL

Sheffield United	1889
Newcastle United	1892
Scunthorpe United	1899
West Ham United	1900
Manchester United	1902
Carlisle United	1904
Southend United	1906
Hartlepool United	1908
Ayr United	1910
Leeds United	1919
Dundee United	1919
Torquay United	1921
Hereford United	1924
Rotheram United	1925
Boston United	1933
Peterborough United	1934
Colchester United	1937
Cambridge United	1951
Oxford United	1960
Airdrie United	2002

The First World Cup

The referee, who wore plus-fours for the match, only agreed to officiate a matter of hours before kick-off, having been assured of his and his fellow officials' safety. Boatloads of Argentinian supporters arriving for the match were searched for arms and, in the earlier rounds, soldiers with fixed bayonets had guarded all the teams. Such was the background to FIFA's inaugural World Cup, staged in Uruguay in 1930.

European representation was weak; only four teams from Europe participated and none of them were seeded. Eight weeks before the competition was due to begin there were still no entries from Europe. It took the intervention of World Cup pioneer, Jules Rimet, to persuade France to enter a team; the Romanian side was handpicked by King Carol himself, who also arranged for the players to have time off work to represent their country. Not surprisingly none of the European teams were seeded. The four seeds were: Argentina, Brazil, Uruguay and the USA.

The first World Cup match was played on 13 July 1930, with France beating Mexico 4–1 and the results followed like this.

Group 1

France	4	Mexico	1
Argentina	1	France	0
Chile	3	Mexico	0
Chile	1	France	0
Argentina	6	Mexico	3
Argentina	3	Chile	1

FOOTBALL

	P	W	D	L	F	A	P
Argentina	3	3	0	0	10	4	6
Chile	3	2	0	1	5	3	4
France	3	1	0	2	4	3	2
Mexico	3	0	0	3	4	13	0

Group 2

Yugoslavia	2	Brazil	1
Yugoslavia	4	Bolivia	0
Brazil	4	Bolivia	0

	P	W	D	L	F	A	P
Yugoslavia	2	2	0	0	6	1	4
Brazil	2	1	0	1	5	2	2
Bolivia	2	0	0	2	0	8	0

Group 3

Romania	3	Peru	1
Uruguay	1	Peru	0
Uruguay	4	Romania	0

	P	W	D	L	F	A	P
Uruguay	2	2	0	0	5	0	4
Romania	2	1	0	1	3	5	2
Peru	2	0	0	2	1	4	0

Group 4

USA	3	Belgium	0				
USA	3	Paraguay	0				
Paraguay	1	Belgium	0				

	P	W	D	L	A	A	P
USA	2	2	0	0	6	0	4
Paraguay	2	1	0	1	1	3	2
Belgium	2	0	0	2	0	4	0

Semi-finals

Argentina	6	USA	1
Uruguay	6	Yugoslavia	1

Final (Montevideo: 30 July 1930. Attendance 90,000)

Uruguay	4	Argentina	2

Man-for-man Marking

As opposed to zonal marking, a player will be assigned an opposition player to mark during the course of a match. If the opposition player goes forward for corners, his man-marker will be expected to accompany him and try and prevent him from getting the ball. Man-for-man marking relies on the player being quicker, sharper and stronger than his opponent if he is to be successful in keeping his opponent quiet during the match.

FOOTBALL

Painting the Arc

The arc, or D, did not appear on the edge of the penalty area on English football pitches until the 1937–8 season. It was introduced to make sure that all other players were at least 10 yards (9m) from the kicker taking a penalty.

Debut Debacle

Irish goalkeeper Tommy Breen had a debut to remember for Manchester United against Leeds in 1936. After just 60 seconds he had his very first touch of the ball – picking it up out of the net having conceded a goal.

Arthur Wharton

Arthur Wharton, the first black professional footballer in Britain, was born in Ghana in 1865 and played in goal for a number of clubs including Preston North End and Sheffield United. Wharton was a remarkable man who ran 100 yards in 10 seconds in 1886, a world record at the time, and who also played professional cricket after his time in football. The biggest moment of his football career came when he played for Preston in the 1887 FA Cup semi–final against West Bromwich Albion – though they lost 3–1.

Goalmouth Incident

During the match between Bournemouth and
Wolverhampton Wanderers on 26 January 1957, Reg
Cutler of Bournemouth collided with a goal post six
minutes into the match and destroyed the goal. The
referee had to stop the game for seven minutes while
the goal was repaired. Though Reg Cutler had the last
laugh; 35 minutes after the restart he scored the only
goal of the match.

Defensive Line-up

'As we say in Portugal, they [Spurs] brought the bus
and they left the bus in front of the goal. I would have
been frustrated if I had been a supporter who paid £50
to watch this game because Spurs came to defend.
There was only one team looking to win, they only
came not to concede – it's not fair for the football we
played.'

José Mourinho

Home Supporters

With disappointing gates for their home games,
Aldershot Town FC sought to explain their poor
following by publishing their version of local
demographics in the programme for the 1953–4 season.

FOOTBALL

Population of Aldershot and District	50000
Less people over 65 not interested in football, have rheumatics or other old age complaints	15000
Less babes in arms and other toddlers	10000
Less people in hospital, lunatic asylums, public houses, services, or otherwise indisposed	8000
Less husbands on allotments or at home doing housework and wives out shopping	12000
People in jail	250
Less shop assistants and others working during football hours	3904
Less gatemen, officials, police and others who do not pay for admission	150
Less people who have acquired complimentary tickets	200
Less people who have climbed over railings	482

Leaving 14: manager, trainer, secretary, 11 players

Just as well that the visitors bring spectators with them!

Fifa's World Ranking

Since the 2006 World Cup the FIFA world rankings, which list national football teams according to performance, have been calculated on the performances in the previous four years; prior to that the calculation period had been the previous eight years.

A points system is used to tabulate performances in international matches recognized by FIFA. These take into account factors such as: the match result; the importance of a match (a friendly carries fewer points than a World Cup encounter); regional strength; the period over which results are collated; and the number of matches considered per year.

In May 2007 the FIFA world rankings were as follows.

1	Italy	12	Croatia
2	Brazil	13	Cameroon
3	Argentina	14	Scotland
4	France	15	Romania
5	Germany	16	Greece
6	The Netherlands	17	Russia
7	Portugal	18	Poland
8	England	19	Turkey
9	Spain	20	Mexico
10	Czech Republic	21	Switzerland
11	Ukraine	22	Sweden

FOOTBALL

23	Denmark	52	Costa Rica
23	Uruguay	53	FYR Macedonia
25	Côte d'Ivoire	54	Burkina Faso
26	Colombia	55	Honduras
27	Nigeria	56	Angola
28	Ghana	57	Hungary
29	USA	58	Uzbekistan
30	Ecuador	59	South Africa
31	Serbia	60	Panama
32	Republic of Ireland	61	Congo DR
33	Northern Ireland	62	Belgium
34	Israel	63	Saudi Arabia
35	Paraguay	64	Belarus
36	Bulgaria	65	Algeria
37	Slovakia	66	Togo
38	Egypt	67	Trinidad & Tobago
39	Senegal	68	Zambia
40	Mali	69	Jamaica
41	Iran	70	Venezuela
42	Australia	71	Cuba
43	Chile	71	Peru
44	Japan	73	China PR
45	Finland	74	Oman
46	Tunisia	75	Wales
47	Morocco	76	Slovenia
48	Bosnia-Herzegovina	77	Austria
49	Norway	78	Albania
50	Guinea	79	Iraq
51	Korea Republic	80	Cyprus

81	Congo	107	Benin
82	Jordan	109	Hong Kong
83	Qatar	110	Estonia
84	Zimbabwe	111	Syria
85	Haiti	112	Malta
86	Equatorial Guinea	113	Barbados
87	Guatemala	114	Sudan
88	Cape Verde Islands	115	Surinam
89	Libya	115	Kazakhstan
90	United Arab Emirates	117	Tanzania
90	Moldova	118	Mozambique
92	Georgia	119	Liberia
92	Lithuania	120	Thailand
94	Canada	121	Burundi
95	Kuwait	122	Rwanda
96	Iceland	123	Bermuda
97	Bolivia	124	Kenya
97	Guyana	125	Singapore
99	Ethiopia	126	Antigua & Barbuda
100	St Vincent and the Grenadines	127	New Zealand
101	Bahrain	128	Armenia
102	Botswana	129	Mauritania
103	Azerbaijan	130	Lebanon
104	Latvia	131	Namibia
104	Gabon	132	Gambia
106	Uganda	133	Chad
107	Malawi	134	Liechtenstein
		134	Yemen
		136	St Kitts & Nevis

FOOTBALL

Mitropa Cup

The Mitropa Cup was the first major international cup for club teams. The name Mitropa is an abbreviation of Mitteleuropa which mean Middle or Central Europe. The competition began in 1927 originally with two teams each from Hungary, Austria, Czechoslovakia and Yugoslavia. The first winner of the competition were Sparta Prague from Czechoslovakia, who beat Rapid Vienna 7–4 over a two-leg final. The scheduled 1940 final between Ferencvárosi from Hungary and Romania's Rapid Bucharest never took place because of the start of the Second World War.

Bolting the Door in Italy

The coach of Inter Milan in the 1960s, Helenio Herrera, is the man most identified with the Italian system of play known as catenaccio. It literally means 'door bolt' and describes the defensive wall approach adopted in Italy – though the concept was created by an Austrian coach Karl Rappan in the 1930s. The system involved four markers at the back with a player, a sweeper, behind them – the door bolt.

Herrera born in Argentina and raised in Morocco demanded total commitment to the cause from his players. He insisted that players swore loyalty to each other before a game, placing their hands on the ball while they gave their oath. The system was remarkably successful for Inter Milan and Herrera, though it came unstuck in the 1967 European Cup Final when they lost to the all-out attacking Celtic side coached by Jock Stein.

Leather on Leather and Leather on Willow

Before the demands on professional sportsmen became as intense as they are today, several notable individuals succeeded in combining their talents as football players with their skill on the cricket field. Ian Botham and Phil Neale are notable examples from more recent times, but they are in fine company, as this list of top-flight cricketing footballers shows.

Ian Botham	Scunthorpe and Somerset
Brian Close	Bradford City and Yorkshire
Denis Compton*	Arsenal and Middlesex
Les Compton	Arsenal and Middlesex

Jimmy Cumbes	West Bromwich Albion and Warwickshire
Andy Ducat*	Arsenal and Kent
Bill Edrich	Tottenham and Middlesex
Walter Hardinge*	Arsenal and Surrey
Ted Helmsley	Sheffield United and Worcestershire
Geoff Hurst	West Ham and Essex
Henry Makepeace*	Everton and Lancashire
Arthur Milton*	Arsenal and Gloucestershire
Phil Neale	Lincoln City, Scunthorpe United and Worcestershire
Ken Taylor	Huddersfield Town and Yorkshire

The starred players earned the rare distinction of becoming double internationals: representing England at both football and cricket. The Compton brothers also achieved a unique double in playing for the cricket County Championship-winning side in the summer and the Football League's champions the following winter (1947–8).

The Reds in Hungary

In 1908 Manchester United decided to celebrate their first League Championship with a quiet end-of-season tour to the Austro–Hungarian Empire. The first match in Vienna went smoothly enough with United winning

FOOTBALL

4–0 against a local combined team. However, the tour hotted up when they arrive in Budapest for two matches against Hungarian team Ferencvaros. United won the first match 6–2, but the second game turned into a diplomatic nightmare.

United, who had scored a record 82 goals in winning the English Championship, continued in their rich vein of form. Initially the partisan crowd applauded the English side's style. But as the game wore on tempers frayed all round. The referee sent off three United players amid a mini-riot (although the referee later relented and let them back on). The police were called and United, with just eight men, finished the game off winning 7–0.

But, as the game ended the locals finally took out their anger on the English players hurling stones from the terraces until they were dispersed by police charging with drawn swords. Nor was the open-top bus they had much help to the United players as it took them back to their hotel, with some of them receiving head injuries from the volley of missiles pelted at them.

Despite profuse apologies from the Hungarian authorities, the Manchester United management vowed never to return to Hungary.

Send on the Subs

Four goalkeepers were used in the England–Wales
international played at Wrexham on 16 March 1908.
Bailey of Leicester Fosse played in the England goal
throughout the game. But the Welsh first-choice
goalkeeper was injured in the first half and was
replaced by the full-back Morris. In the second half
England allowed the Welsh to bring on Davies of
Bolton to replace Morris.

For Club and Country

When Matt Busby was in charge of Manchester United
in 1958 he was also part-time manager of Scotland;
while his assistant coach at United Jimmy Murphy was
managing the Welsh national side. Both teams got to
the 1958 World Cup finals

Victory by Default

In 1920 Belgium became the last host nation to win the
Olympic football tournament in one of the most
controversial incidents in Olympic history. In the final
they played Czechoslovakia who, having had a player
sent off, failed to get satisfaction from the English
referee, John Lewis, walked off the pitch and were
disqualified. As a consequence the title was awarded to
Belgium by default.

FOOTBALL

The First League Cup

The League Cup was introduced into English football at the start of the 1960s and was open to all 92 League clubs. The first final played over two legs in 1961 was won 3–2 by Aston Villa who beat Second Division Rotherham after extra time in the second leg. Some leading clubs including Arsenal, Sheffield Wednesday, Tottenham Hotspur, West Bromwich Albion and Wolverhampton Wanderers refused to take part.

Down and Out

In the 1930 World Cup in Uruguay the US team physio needed help himself after collapsing on the pitch in the semi-final between the USA and Argentina, which was played on 26 July. The trainer had gone onto the pitch to treat one of his injured players. But he was still upset about a controversial goal scored by Argentina and chucked down his medical bag in a huff. Alas, this broke the bottle of chloroform inside, the trainer was overcome by the fumes – and his players had to drag him off the pitch. Things got even worse as the USA went down 6–1 to their South American opponents.

Identity Crisis

French club Union Sportive thought they had come up with a cunning solution when one of their star players Charlie Wetzel had to go off injured in a match with Bataville in 1967. At half-time they secretly put on Wetzel's identical twin brother Claude to avoid playing with ten men. Inevitably perhaps Claude equalized and became the team hero – at least until the final whistle.

Sadly for Union Sportive, the deception was spotted at the end of the match and Bataville were awarded the points – and poor old Claude received a suspension.

Italian Fans

Nottingham Forest can claim real revolutionary pedigree for their club colour. The Reds were founded in 1865 and one of the first things the new club did was to buy 12 red caps, complete with tassels. The colour was in honour of the great Italian revolutionary Giuseppe Garibaldi, whose men were famously known as Redshirts. Garibaldi, whose exploits helped bring about the unification of Italy, was a popular figure among many people in Britain at the time.

Championship Material

Since the Premiership trophy replaced the old First Division title in English football in 1992–3, only four clubs have won it and none of them have been led by an English manager. As the roll of honour shows, two winning managers are Scots, one is French and the fourth is Portuguese.

Year	Club	Manager
1992–3	Manchester United	Alex Ferguson
1993–4	Manchester United	Alex Ferguson
1994–5	Blackburn Rovers	Kenny Dalglish
1995–6	Manchester United	Alex Ferguson
1996–7	Manchester United	Alex Ferguson
1997–8	Arsenal	Arsène Wenger
1998–9	Manchester United	Alex Ferguson
1999–0	Manchester United	Alex Ferguson
2000–1	Mancheser United	Alex Ferguson
2001–2	Arsenal	Arsène Wenger
2002–3	Manchester United	Alex Ferguson
2003–4	Arsenal	Arsène Wenger
2004–5	Chelsea	José Mourinho
2005–6	Chelsea	José Mourinho
2006–7	Manchester United	Alex Ferguson

Coincidence, Coincidence

The future England World Cup-winning manager, Alf Ramsey, signed for Southampton Football Club on the same day in 1942 as fellow player Harry Evans. Thirteen years later, on 9 August 1955, they both became managers for the first time when Ramsey was appointed to take charge of Ipswich Town and Evans became manager of Aldershot.

Double Standards

For many years the English FA regarded their fixtures against Scotland as far more important than those against Wales and Ireland. Often the sides picked to play against the Welsh or Irish consisted of players who couldn't get into the team against the Scots. In 1893 it was decided that England would pick two teams, one amateur, one professional, who would play against Wales or Ireland. From these sides they would then select the best XI to play Scotland.

Law v Banks

Denis Law scored against the great goalkeeper Gordon Banks for three different teams at Wembley. These were for Manchester United in the FA Cup in 1963, for the Rest of the World against England in the same year and for Scotland against England in 1965 and 1967.

Long-serving Managers

In June 2007 20 managers of Football League Clubs had managed the same club for three or more seasons. Their 'roll of honour' read as follows.

Manager	Club	Appointed/ Duration
1 Dario Gradi	Crewe Alexandra	June 1983 24 seasons

FOOTBALL

2 Sir Alex Ferguson	Manchester United	Nov 1986 21 seasons
3 Graham Turner	Hereford United	August 1995 12 seasons
4 Arsène Wenger	Arsenal	Sept 1996 11 seasons
5 John Coleman	Accrington Stanley	August 1999 8 seasons
6 Steve Bruce	Birmingham City	Dec 2001 6 seasons
7 David Moyes	Everton	March 2002 5 seasons
8 Martin Ling	Leyton Orient	Sept 2003 4 seasons
9 Steve Coppell	Reading	October 2003 4 seasons
10 John Ward	Cheltenham Town	Nov 2003 4 seasons
11 Steve Tllson	Southend United	Nov 2003 4 seasons
12 Martin Foyle	Port Vale	Feb 2004 3 seasons
13 Steve Evans	Boston United	Feb 2004 3 seasons
14 Paul Fairclough	Barnet	March 2004 3 seasons
15 José Mourinho	Chelsea	June 2004 3 seasons

16 Steve Cotterill	Burnley	June 2004
		3 seasons
17 Rafael Benitez	Liverpool	June 2004
		3 seasons
18 Mark Hughes	Blackburn Rovers	Sept 2004
		3 seasons
19 Martin Jol	Tottenham Hotspur	Nov 2004
		3 seasons
20 Gary Peters	Shrewsbury Town	Nov 2004
		3 seasons

Away-goals Rule

Rangers' attempt to win the European Cup Winners' Cup in 1972 seemed to have gone horribly wrong in the second round against Sporting Lisbon. At the end of the second leg in Portugal the aggregate score stood at 6–6. On the night, Rangers had lost 4–3 and the referee ordered a penalty shoot-out – which the Glasgow team lost.

But manager Willie Waddell pointed to the rule book, which said that away goals counted double – and Rangers had scored more goals away than Sporting Lisbon. Thanks to his timely intervention Rangers were duly awarded the tie and went on to win the Cup that year.

FOOTBALL

Blame the Ref

A Spurs–Huddersfield League match in 1952 saw one of the most controversial goals ever scored in the history of the Football League. Eddie Bailey let fly a re-taken Spurs corner, which hit the referee on the back before rebounding to Bailey, who chipped it to Len Duquemin, allowing him to score the only goal of the match.

The Huddersfield players were suitably incensed and protested to the referee that Bailey had played the ball twice before it had touched another player, which was against the rules, but the unsighted referee and the League allowed the disputed goal to stand.

Better Late Than Never?

William Henry Carr must have been hoping for a long England career after he was selected to play in goal for his country against Scotland at the Kennington Oval on 6 March 1875. However, the player from the Owlerton club in Sheffield missed his train down to the capital and only arrived after the match had been under way for 15 minutes.

Fortunately for Carr, England had let in no goals. Unfortunately for Carr, by full-time he had let in two goals in a 2–2 draw. He never played for England again.

The Pride of Scotland

The Scottish Football Association International Roll of Honour was inaugurated in February 1988 when the first 11 Scottish players to have won 50 international caps were placed on the roll. Since then the number of players has increased to the point that by June 2007 there were 25 names.

Each player honoured in this way receives a gold medal and his portrait is hung in the Scottish Football Museum.

Player	Caps	International Career	Clubs
Kenny Dalglish	102	1971–1986	Celtic Liverpool
Jim Leighton	91	1982–1998	Aberdeen (twice) Manchester Utd Hibernian
Alex McLeish	77	1980–1993	Aberdeen
Paul McStay	76	1983–1997	Celtic
Tom Boyd	72	1990–2001	Motherwell Chelsea Celtic
Willie Miller	65	1975–1989	Aberdeen
Christian Dailly	65	1997–	Blackburn Rvrs Derby County West Ham Utd

FOOTBALL

Danny McGrain	62	1973–1982	Celtic
Richard Gough	61	1983–1993	Dundee United
			Tottenham H'spur
			Rangers
Ally McCoist	61	1985–1998	Rangers
			Kilmarnock
John Collins	58	1988–1999	Hibernian
			Celtic
			AS Monaco
			Everton
Roy Aitken	57	1979–1991	Celtic
			St Mirren
Gary McAllister	57	1990–1999	Leicester City
			Leeds United
			Coventry City
David Weir	56	1997–	Heart of Mid'an
			Everton
			Rangers
Denis Law	55	1958–1974	Huddersfield Tn
			Manchester City
			(twice)
			Torino
			Manchester Utd
Maurice Malpas	55	1984–1992	Dundee United
Billy Bremner	54	1965–1975	Leeds United
Graeme Souness	54	1974–1986	Middlesbrough
			Liverpool
			Sampdoria
			Rangers

George Young	53	1946–1957	Rangers
Alan Rough	53	1976–1986	Partick Thistle
			Hibernian
Kevin Gallacher	53	1988–2001	Dundee United
			Coventry City
			Blackburn Rovers
			Newcastle United
Joe Jordan	52	1973–1982	Leeds United
			Manchester Utd
			Milan AC
Colin Hendry	51	1993–2001	Blackburn Rovers
			Rangers
			Coventry City
			Bolton Wanderers
Asa Hartford	50	1972–1982	West Bromwich Albion
			Manchester City
			Everton
Gordon Strachan	50	1980–1992	Aberdeen
			Manchester Utd
			Leeds United

Everton of Anfield

Despite the long association of Liverpool FC with Anfield, Everton FC were in fact the first football club to play at the famous ground. Everton rented a field in Anfield Road to play its games until there was a split in the club over rent for the ground. One part of the club retained the name Everton, but moved home to take up residence at Goodison Park, leaving the other part to continue playing at Anfield under the new name of Liverpool Association FC.

Worth Every Penny

In February 1979 the Birmingham City and England striker, Trevor Francis, made headline news when he became the first player sold between English football clubs for £1 million. The transfer fee itself amounted £999,999; reputedly, Forest manager Brian Clough had pegged it £1 short of the magic million because he did not want the landmark fee to go his new signing's head. (When additional sums were added – VAT, the contribution to the Football League Provident Fund and the Francis's own cut – the total sum paid by Nottingham Forest was £1,180,00.)

That season Forest were the reigning League champions and League Cup holders, but registration regulations prevented Francis from playing any part his new club's retention of the League Cup, neither was he allowed to join their European Cup campaign until the semi-finals. Having secured their place in the final, Forest travelled to Munich to take on Swedish side Malmö.

In the eyes of Forest fans, the colossal investment the club had made in England's record-breaking signing was repaid close to half time. After gaining possession of the ball, Brian Clough's team moved it wide to the left of the field, where it was skilfully taken to the byline by winger John Robertson, who curled back an outswinging cross towards the far post. Trevor Francis had spotted this and was racing to intercept the ball, though even he ended up throwing himself headlong to take it low to the ground, before heading it high into the roof of the Malmö net. That was the only goal of the match and it won Brian Clough and his players the European Cup that year.

The image of Trevor Francis stooping to connect with his winning header became a memorable icon of the club's success at Nottingham Forest's City Ground and for several years afterwards it formed part of the opening titles of Match of the Day.

Brought to Book

On 19 January 1991, the then Sheffield United player, Vinnie Jones, was booked within five seconds of play beginning in a match against Manchester City. A little over twelve months later, when he was playing for Chelsea, Jones beat his own record by being booked after three seconds, when the ball was still in the centre circle.

His opponents that afternoon? Sheffield United.

FOOTBALL

Soccer

Despite its use in North America, where 'soccer' distinguishes 'association football' from the indigenous game of football, the word 'soccer' originated in the UK in the 19th century. In fact it was derived from the official name of the sport – association football – which in turn took its name from the sport's governing body in England: the Football Association.

Since referring to the game by its full name was something of a mouthful, the syllable formed by three middle letters of As–soc–iation gave rise to the word 'soc'. In the same way that the name 'rugger' evolved from Rugby Football, 'Soc' had '-er tagged to its ending (with an additional 'c') to create 'soccer'.

Back to Back Goals

On 15 March 1952, Aldershot reserves were playing Millwall reserves at the Dell. In goal for Aldershot was Fred Brown, who suffered the double embarrassment of twice drop-kicking the ball, only to see it strike the back of Millwall forward Jimmy Constantine and rebound into the net on both occasions. Those two freak goals led to Aldershot losing 4–1, but they probably helped Brown in his development as a goalkeeper, because he turned professional and went on to play for West Bromwich Albion and Portsmouth.

Jumping to it

The 1998 World Cup finals in France witnessed at least one innovative addition the footballer's wide portfolio of skills and tricks. This was demonstrated by the Mexican winger Cuauhtemoc Blanco, who found his way through a determined South Korean defence on two occasions when he wedged the ball between his feet and jumped – heralding the arrival of what was quickly named the 'Blanco Bounce'.

Escape to Victory

The 1981 Second World War film, Escape to Victory, brings together a cast of celebrated film actors and a number of world-famous football players. The plot reaches its climax when a team of Allied prisoners escape captivity during a match played against a team representing Germany.

The team members in the cast include the following 'stars'.

Character	Actor/Player	Career
Erik Ball	Søren Lindsted	Danish player for Belgian clubs: Genk and Liège
Terry Brady	Bobby Moore	International: England Captain

FOOTBALL

Doug Clure John Colby	Russell Osman Michael Caine	International: England Double Oscar winner
Corporal Luis Fernandez	Pelé	International: Brazil
Michel Fileu	Paul Van Himst	International: Belgium
Sid Harmor	Mike Summerbee	International: England
Captain Robert Hatch	Sylvester Stallone	Double Oscar nominee
Arthur Hayes	John Wark	International: Scotland
Gunnar Hilsson	Hallvar Thoresen	International: Norway
Carlos Rey	Osvaldo Ardiles	International: Argentina
Paul Wolchek	Kazimierz Deyna	International: Poland
Pieter Van Beck	Co Prins	Dutch player for Ajax and FC Kaiserslautern

Come on England!

During Euro 96 thousands of Scots fans began cheering on England in one of the most unexpected displays of support ever witnessed in international football.

However, there was more than a degree of self-interest in their enthusiasm for the 'old enemy'. Scotland were playing Switzerland at Villa Park, where they were struggling to extend their 1–0 lead in order to progress to the quarter finals. England, playing in the same group as Scotland, were leading Holland at Wembley. As radio commentary, listened to avidly at Villa Park, broadcast England goals flying in and as the score line rose to four England goals to none for their Dutch opponents, it looked as if England's winning margin might be sufficient to take Scotland with them to the next stage as group runners-up. Then the Dutch spoilt it all, scored a late consolation goal, and went through ahead of Scotland on goal difference.